God Bless Our Queer Old Dean

W. STORRS LEE

God Bless

Our Queer Old Dean

G. P. PUTNAM'S SONS

New York

© 1959 BY W. STORRS LEE

All rights reserved. This book, or parts
thereof, must not be reproduced in any form
without permission.

Published simultaneously in the Dominion of
Canada by Longmans, Green & Co., Toronto.

The Library of Congress has cataloged this book as follows:

Lee, William Storrs. God bless our queer old dean.
  New York, Putnam [1959] 253 p. illus. 22 cm.
  1. Deans (in schools) I. Title. LB2341.L28 378.11
  59-5679 ‡

MANUFACTURED IN THE UNITED STATES OF AMERICA

To THE HUNDREDS OF STUDENTS *who were in and out of the Dean's Office at Middlebury College between 1945 and 1955—the invited and the uninvited, the Phi Betes and the flunks, the resolute war veterans and the less eager warriors in ROTC, the complainers and the compliant, the scapegoats and the scapegraces, those with honest grievances and those with more speculative gripes, the creators of ingenious excuses and the forthright souls lacking that kind of imagination, the troubled and the troublemakers, the hellions and the oh-so-helpfuls, and particularly to that handful of undergraduates who were always ready to accept a responsible and intelligent partnership in the conduct of student affairs—student allies without whom no dean could survive for a semester.*

For their generous assistance the author is deeply grateful to

Dean Mark Almli, St. Olaf College

Dean Philip S. Ambrose, New Mexico College of Agriculture and Mechanic Arts

Dean Frank C. Baldwin, Cornell University

Professor W. H. Cowley, Stanford University

Dean and Mrs. William G. Craig, Stanford University

Dean Clifford J. Craven, University of Oklahoma

Associate Dean Leo R. Dowling, Indiana University

Dean Edward J. Durnall, Jr., Nasson College

Dean Donald M. DuShane, University of Oregon

Dean Joseph E. Gould, State University of New York Teachers College, Fredonia

Dean Milton L. Hinga, Hope College

Dean John E. Hocutt, University of Delaware

Dean W. Dean Holdeman, Oberlin College

Dean Robert S. Hopkins, Jr., University of Massachusetts

Professor Amos B. Horlacher, Dickinson College

Associate Dean Eugene Hotchkiss, Dartmouth College

Dean Merrill E. Jarchow, Carleton College

Dean Nathaniel C. Kendrick, Bowdoin College

Dean Arthur H. Kiendl, University of Colorado

Dean Charles L. Lewis, University of North Dakota

Director John U. Monro, Financial Aid Office, Harvard

Vice President John F. Morse, Rensselaer Polytechnic Institute

Vice President Frank P. Piskor, Syracuse University

Dean Ann W. Shepard, Reed College

President Robert M. Strozier, Florida State University

Dean Fred H. Turner, University of Illinois

President Robert C. Weller, Mitchell College

CONTENTS

THE DEAN AT WORK
—AND PLAY

*A Preface by Robert M. Strozier**

THERE have been no periods of normality in higher education during the last forty years. The campus disruption brought on by World War I faded into the rip-roaring '20s. Came the depression and everything changed again. Then just as the classroom was beginning to come to order at last, far-off wars and rumors of near conflict led students off on a tussle with their consciences as to whether or not they would be induced to participate in any warfare. Hardly were the pledges of pacifism dry on the paper before the pacifists were in uniform and the curriculum and college calendar were altered to accommodate the army and navy of World War II. The GIs coming back after 1945 upset the applecart by insisting upon mature purpose in education. When the veterans thinned out, the youngsters who had been mingling with them thought that they were entitled to all the adult concessions like respectable cars, marriage, and academic independ-

* Dr. Strozier is President of Florida State University. This preface was in part first presented as an address before the 1958 conference of the National Association of Student Personnel Administrators.

13

ence—without so much emphasis on the educational purpose. A brief bust was followed by Sputnik and a recession. Few deans—very few—have survived the cataclysms.

And since dean's offices were just beginning to open up four decades back, no living dean has ever known a period of normality and no student has ever known a "normal" dean. During these forty years of constant change, the deans have carried a little bit more than their share of the responsibilities and when things were rough, they have too frequently been blamed for circumstances which were far beyond their control.

What is a dean of students and what is a student? We cannot set up in Platonic fashion a standard for an ideal dean of students or an ideal student. Both are products of two forces bigger than they: (1) the society, containing influential institutions beyond the college such as family and church, and (2) the college, in which the faculty, administration, and board really predetermine what kind of guy the dean may be and what his relations to students may be.

In one sense we may say that a dean of students who is in constant crisis in his relationships with his students is himself, personally, intellectually and emotionally in constant crisis; that any judgment a dean of students makes about his student body really is a judgment of himself.

Perhaps a dean of students is not the one to describe a good student or a bad student. He probably feels elated about most students on some days and, on others, considers the majority of them young monsters. The morning that the college newspaper points out the inadequacies of the administration and of the dean more particularly, he wonders why it would not be better to have a training school in which young people were told what to do and say and were not inspired to be independent thinkers. In fact, it would be simpler. We ask our students to reason, to accept nothing at face value, to think of the best solutions to problems idealistically as well as practically. When they do just that, we are likely to recoil from the unpleasantness of their doing so.

We may say that a dean's critical, if not impossible, task is to understand sensitively the tensions implicit in his society and college. For example, a dean who cannot understand and appreciate what the national pressure to produce scientists will mean to countless hundreds of pliable young people is unfit. A dean who cannot react with understanding to the confusion and intellectual paralysis now gripping many college presidents who must continue to deal with public opinion during this "crisis" really is unfit too.

In a dean's relations with students a college really comes to the firing line of all the national and international currents beating against the concept "higher education." This forum is no protected faculty meeting, no closed-door session of the president and his staff. This forum is real. It is the forum through which a terrifying number of crucial judgments about the whole college are made.

What is a student? The thirst for knowledge is the essential ingredient, the ingredient which excludes from this charmed circle many persons who are registered and following courses in college.

We must also exclude the young dilettantes who are sent by their parents for a little polish or to pass four awkward years between adolescence and physical maturity and vocation.

We must exclude the young intellectual who resents all organized society, who considers himself beyond and above his fellow students.

We must omit the person who has been so sheltered and disciplined in his youth that he is afraid to attack new ideas. If his father has decided that he will be a laywer, he will be a lawyer—although he would much prefer to study literature.

There are many who are real students. Nothing appeals to me more than a green freshman, and nothing less than one who considers himself sophisticated. Meeting eager youths every fall gives one the courage to go on, while visiting alumni groups is sometimes dispiriting.

Independence in students is, however, a subtle concept. We would be less than honest to suggest that private or public education in this country is completely independent. All education is fundamentally responsible to public opinion. Too often, alas, the educational institutions may follow rather than lead public opinion. Thus the basic concept that the college stands *in loco parentis*—a concept which I accept—may be mistaken to mean that we should continue to treat as adolescents young men and women whom we should be assisting to become mature citizens. The tension between complete freedom and responsibility calls upon the talents and training of the personnel administrator. The very fact that we accept a responsibility to help students to maturity differentiates our institutions from most of those in other countries where this responsibility is not considered within the province of the university.

Since colleges have assumed this role, the dean at work is faced with every kind of problem. To take as an example the health of students, he may be asked to decide whether student health should offer care of the teeth and eyesight of students, psychoanalysis for the disturbed (or if not psychoanalysis, how much psychiatric care), where psychologists may be used instead of psychiatrists, whether Christian Scientists should be exempt from preventive medicine or from any health rules of the university, how much hospitalization is to be allowed, what is to be done with the foreign student who proves to be tubercular after he has arrived on scholarship for two years, whether the suspected homosexual should be immediately separated from the student body or given therapy—and on and on. Solomon's decision about the mother of that baby seems relatively simple.

The dean at work flounders in frustration unless he, in cooperation with the administration of the school, has determined with imaginative precision and preceptive logic his role in the total life and organization of the university. It requires no prophetic vision to observe that many deans spend time and energy with problems which are external to the actual administration of their offices. The reason for this imbalance may lie with the administration which views the dean's duties as external to the arterial system of the institution.

He may be viewed as the major-domo of a side show while others in the school carry on inside the big top. He

17

may operate a glorified lost-and-found department, attempting to gather together all the loose threads of miscellaneous offices which somehow find their way into an educational institution. Or he may be the morale officer, the one who is supposed to be present and calm in time of crisis (there are always crises) and avert disaster as well as damage to institutional property.

For the best interests of the dean and of the institution, there must be some basic assumptions: (1) That the educational institution has solved or is solving its real problem, that of the aim and destiny of the institution; (2) That the dean is an integral part of the administration of the school where there obtains an equilibrium of forces similar to what the economist calls "perfect competition"; (3) That there are clearly established services for students, grouped under the dean and his staff, who are given adequate authority to grapple with them.

We workers in the vineyard have long recognized these as basic principles and have attempted to educate the presidents, when they are educable, of the necessity of accepting them. Many of the presidents accept them in what is often lightly called "principle" and then with omniscience and omnipotence render decisions which negate the very basis on which the dean is working. These are occupational hazards in the dean's work, and so long as vanity and lack of guts remain human frailties, there is not much hope for presidents. The smart dean is one who can make a polite *no* sound like *hell no,* so that it does not occur to the student, parent, or patron to go to the president anyway.

I have the distinct premonition from all the present

talk about the teachers' colleges and their soft curricula that the dean may be working in new fields before too long; that is, attempting to save from the inquiring minds of the profane those things which we have worked so long to establish. The satellite program both here and in Russia has caused a kind of uneasiness on the part of the general public concerning the schools. It is needless to recount here what they have been saying about *life adjustment* courses in the high schools and colleges. Unfortunately, a good bit of it is true. Those who did not understand John Dewey and who sought to follow his principles without his wisdom have brought some strange dishes to the educational table. Too often we find a meal with hors d'oeuvres, salads, and desserts but no meat and potatoes. As a professor of romance languages, I have been impressed by the statistics published on the study of foreign languages both here and abroad. To learn that eight thousand Americans are studying Russian while ten million Russians are studying English is a sobering thought. It pleases our vanity to know that English is considered so important, but we are aware that the Russians are not studying our language in order to understand the subtleties of *Hamlet* or to join the millions who have secretly enjoyed *Peyton Place*. Their aims are obviously to advance their own interests. I should wish that all our students know well one foreign language, first for its esthetic values, but also for its use in understanding better our own language. That there are practical uses for a foreign language in business and in diplomacy is obvious, yet this is an area of study that has been increasingly reduced in high schools and colleges.

19

The science and mathematics areas have been the center of the discussion, although some strange characters in the educational world have given lip service to the humanities and the social sciences in the endless discussions and papers on the subject of Sputnik.

These, however, are not our prime concern today. We must foresee where these discussions inevitably lead. When John Dewey's statue has finally been removed and Don Bestor is proclaimed king, then the "personnel point of view" may be the subject of additional scrutiny, both by deans and others. The crucial thing now is not how the dean of students may be viewed by *others*, but how he professionally looks at himself. The interesting question, the answer to which deans of students jolly well better think about, is whether or not there really is an incompatibility between Don Bestor's position and the "personnel point of view."

Like most educators, we are prone to prolixity and vagueness about our objectives, as well as the means of accomplishing them. We often are guilty of busywork when important needs are neglected. And the very jargon we use often obfuscates instead of clarifying.

The dean whose administration includes responsibility for academic counseling now must reconsider his whole apparatus, and the substantive question now raised is whether the crucial academic counseling should take place at the junior or senior high school level rather than at the undergraduate level.

For the dean whose administration does not include academic counseling, a somewhat different challenge is presented: how can he continue to administer the extracurriculum and his other services during this time of re-examination without establishing some new relationship between his own enterprise and the academic side of student life?

Administrators at all levels have a difficult role in the academic community. An administrator is supposed to get things done. But too often I fear we become so absorbed in doing things that we lose sight of the primary objectives of the college or university. Sometimes we act too much like corporation executives rather than like teachers. We must be both. Too rarely do we combine in ourselves the necessary ingredients of scholarship and administrative ability. Yet, an administrator who has no claim to scholarship cannot act with poise and security in an educational environment. Neither the technical jargon we have developed in our fields nor the slick techniques we sometimes take for panaceas can replace the qualification of sound academic training. The issue is much broader than the mere achievement of academic respectability. Respectability in the academic community is a vague concept, too often used to conceal qualities unbecoming to those who teach. Competence, not respectability, is the issue.

My concern is not for top administrators, but for those who make the wheels turn, lest they become little more than stokers at the intellectual furnace. The main business of the college is teaching, and that of a university both teaching and research. These solid facts we should never forget. Education does not end in the classroom; it begins there, and the educational process should permeate the whole life of the campus. The residence halls, the extracurriculum, the sports programs, the publications, all should be an integral part of the educative process—but they are only a part, and let's face it, the second part. The classroom remains the core of our enterprise. The college could go on without the extracurriculum. The curriculum is indispensable.

The educational values of the extracurriculum cannot be realized unless we understand, and are closely allied with, the curriculum itself—unless the force of our work is felt and favorably received by the members of the academic community who are solely academic in their interests and pursuits.

The dean out of his office is something else again. Many of them are astonishingly convivial once they leave their own little work orbits and are seen whirling in outer space. Some of these same men are stuffed shirts on their own campuses.

We all get tired of administration. We become excessively tired when we drone on day after day, convinced of the necessity of our presence at all times, unable to delegate responsibility, and smug in the belief in our own ability to solve problems alone.

The ability of an administrator to recruit a first-class staff and to delegate authority is the true test of his effectiveness. The dean should be able not only to spend some time in quiet reflection about his problems, but also to play with the assurance that he will be called when there is a real crisis which demands his particular authority. Some of the most tiresome administrators are those who pride themselves on never taking a vacation. They may snatch a week end here or perhaps a week there, but they are always about, sure that their physical presence is sufficient to calm the president, impress the faculty, and suggest to the trustees that they are the real backbone of the institution and naturally vastly unappreciated and underpaid.

Every dean should have at least one month of consecutive vacation. During the first week he will unwind; during the second he will begin to realize that the other administrators also have problems, and that the tempest in his own staff between the assistant dean and the director is not as important as it seemed when he was on campus; during the remainder of the time he will have a vacation and gain some perspective on the problems of his campus. Many of them are, after all, quite trivial.

All the other virtues of the dean take second place to his naturalness and sincerity with his staff and with the students. The trustees and the president can be fooled with busywork and sometimes with insincerity; even the staff is, at times, taken in, but the students, never. They seem to have a sixth sense which accurately gauges the extent of sincerity, and they have their own methods of rejecting those who fail them. They are understanding of human frailty but never of the slick answer, assumed piety, false dignity, or phony comradeship. The dean who seeks their approbation by the "Just call me Jim" method is heading for real trouble. The students want friendship, but they don't want a pal. They want to respect the dean, but for what he is, not for what he would like to think of himself. They are not displeased to know he can also play, provided he is not a delayed adolescent who cannot find his place with his peers.

In my eleven years as Dean of Students at the University of Chicago I had a taste of everything, and when I say everything I mean everything. At times the taste seemed to be a sea of troubles in which I was swimming without direction, like the lost air pilot who said boastfully that he did not know where he was going but that he was making good time. I feel sure that those years gave me a fuller comprehension of the role of the dean. And now, as the president of a university, I find that I expect nothing of my dean but that he perform with unobtrusive perfection.

1.

"WHAT, PRAY, IS ALL

THIS DEANERIE ABOUT?"

RANDY CLOSED the door to the inner sanctum, crossed the rug toward the dean's desk, and drew a revolver.

"Well, this is it," he announced, leveling the .38. He released the safety catch.

There are a great many extremists who think all deans should voluntarily queue up before a well-equipped firing squad and submit to the inevitable—without waiting until sunrise—but the man looking into the barrel of that revolver was a good guy; he was not expendable. Moreover, for a year and a half he had ranked his assailant as an amiable, level-headed lad, the last one in his class likely to lose touch with reality. To cope with such staggering surprises is one of the reasons deans are rewarded with more ample stipends than their academic colleagues, stipends sometimes totaling as much as six thousand a year—or less.

Undoubtedly the dean would have died then, but with a resounding thud someone in the outer office spilled an armful of books at that moment and the genial assassin glanced around uneasily to make sure that the door was going to remain closed until the deed was done.

In that split second, the dean could have pressed his buzzer and signaled an SOS to his secretary, but, he thought, why encourage a further reduction in the college ranks? Besides, the move would have only hastened his own end. Instead he resigned himself to the worst, tipped back in his chair, and made a supreme effort to belie the appearance of a man without apprehension. The clear case of checkmate was not to be denied, although his instincts for self-preservation were abandoned with reluctance.

He was used to having students burst in upon him with the pronouncement, "I got a problem." Now, for the life of him, all he could think of was the inadequate echo, "What's your problem, Randy?"

"It's your problem, not mine," assured Randy blandly —almost sympathetically. "This has been due for a long time."

Then, as if he had decided there was no hurry about the execution after all, he trustingly placed the revolver on the edge of the desk, turned his back, and swung around a chair in which to seat himself. The maneuver provided just time enough for the dean to snatch the weapon; but with reckless nonchalance he resisted the temptation. A glance was all he gave it. He noted that it was a Smith and Wesson and the cylinder was fully loaded.

The pleasant sophomore seated himself and leaned forward with crossed arms on the desk. There was nothing

evasive about him, no shifty eye, no sign of nervousness. He was completely straightforward, as though doing away with the dean were a distasteful business, but in line with his prescribed duty. To emphasize that impression, he thoughtfully moved the revolver to the center of the desk where it would be equally accessible to both parties. The dean took the liberty of shoving it back an inch.

"Yup, this is it," Randy reminded himself uncertainly.

The dean was racking his brain for a famous last word or for small talk that would serve as a stall. Oh, yes, Randy was the boy who liked to write those innocuous letters to the editor. "That was a good argument you had in the *Daily* last week," he said smoothly, "the piece about fair play and campus politics."

"Keeping everything on the level. That's my idea," Randy acknowledged matter-of-factly. "Fair play, no favor, as they say."

How could an unhinged mind work so confidently and so coherently, the dean wondered. He wished he could dredge up some clue as to what had set the boy off, but he didn't know where or how to begin. It could be an accumulation of invented anxieties—courses going badly, trouble with a girl, finances, affairs at home. Whatever was bothering him evidently had to be focused on one person as the ultimate cause, and the dean as usual was the victim. He was sure the youngster was beyond the stage where a dean's amateur ferreting would yield much.

"Sorry to have to do it this way," Randy apologized, getting back to the purpose of his mission. He patted the revolver. "But there is one big thing I want to settle first, one point on which we ought to come to an understanding—"

He faltered, flushed deeply, and was silent. To his utter embarrassment, that one point escaped him.

"But two people can't settle an argument with one pistol," suggested the dean philosophically from the depths of his inclined chair. "Both parties have to have an equal advantage. Keep things on the level, as you say."

That was a new slant. "You're right," the student allowed after a moment of tangled thought. "We ought to have fair play. You need a gun too. Where is it? In your desk?"

"No, unfortunately I don't own one," replied the dean.

To the boy with the .38, this shortage of weapons suddenly posed another insurmountable obstacle, more overwhelming than all the problems confusing his muddled brain. For the first time he looked bewildered and cast a cloudy look at the dean.

Three quarters of an hour later Randy was en route to the office of the university psychiatrist and the pistol was in the dean's desk drawer—with the safety catch on.

The dean didn't collapse after his ordeal. He didn't bother to notify the president. To spare his secretary any alarm, he didn't even mention the incident to her. His phone conversations with the psychiatrist were his only communication. Besides, there wasn't time for gloating over his lucky survival. The bench in the outer office was filled with students waiting to see him. One corner of his desk was piled a foot high with faculty reports he had to assimilate and condense into a few paragraphs of his own before a committee met that afternoon; on another corner was a stack of forms from the treasurer's office which his secretary had twice reminded him had to be reviewed and signed that day; and in his basket was a three-inch miscellany of morning mail which he wanted to take care of before noon. But the paper work held no priority so long as there were students waiting for consultation on their pressing emergencies.

The next teaser was brought in by a distraught junior who desperately needed to be excused from his French class to catch a bus for Boston. His hypothesis was obscure, something to do with a fraternity brother's having had the gall to date his steady without permission. In retaliation, the victim was considering busting out of his fraternity, but first he had to make a trip to Wellesley to square things there. The dean decided not to get involved; Beta Chi, Wellesley, and a cooling-off period would take care of the dilemma better than he could. Referring to timetables, he patiently pointed out that a bus leaving a half-hour after the class would get to Boston in plenty of time. Choking with resentment over the dean's failure to sense the seriousness of his plight, the junior stomped out muttering that he'd have to leave on the first bus anyway and take the consequences of cutting the class.

Gloomily the dean drew a letter from the top of his "In" basket and scanned enough of the first paragraph to see that it was a philippic from a distinguished alumnus wanting to know why the grandson of a friend of his law partner had been turned down by the admissions office. There wasn't time to read the second and third pages. Glancing up, he brightened to see cheerful Mike Sikolski standing in the doorway. Mike was redrafting the constitution of the Big B Society. He was one of the considerate boys who always apologized for intruding and taking so much time on matters that really were relatively important; a hardworking, intelligent kingpin of the campus, representing the steady minority who make life bearable for college administrators, Mike was stuck with a clause of Article II, Section C, dealing with faculty representation in the society, and needed a word of wisdom from higher authority. He got his answer promptly, apologized again, and withdrew.

The dean kept his temper while dressing down three roommates who were making life intolerable for their neighbors in Forsythe Hall, and lost it temporarily ten minutes later while interrogating a sullen young bruiser who had reportedly slept seven females in his room the previous night. Caught in a lie, the roué declined to talk, so the dean decided to let him sweat it out for a while, and requested him to drop in at his home that evening. Good Lord, he recalled as the boy was leaving, he had promised to take his wife out to dinner and the movies, the first date they had had in months. Well, some other time.

Following a distressing long-distance call from a Bridgeport hospital, he was obliged to summon a freshman and break the news about the complications resulting from his father's operation: chances of pulling through weren't good. The dean worked out the quickest route home for the boy, loaned him a ten-dollar bill, accompanied him to the front door of the Administration Building, and saw him off reflecting a brave smile.

Between other phone calls, an argumentative youngster from Alabama, with a remarkable talent for massacring the English tongue, stormed in to explain that the new foreign language requirement proposed by the faculty was not only unreasonable and illegal, but also un-American. Another called to find out why it was necessary for the university always to serve cold fried eggs for breakfast. A chemistry professor pushed in ahead of two undergraduates to announce triumphantly that one of his majors had ingeniously isolated something or other in the lab; thinking of the faculty reports and the committee meeting coming up, the dean really couldn't care less, but he warmly congratulated the professor and made a note to send an appropriate memo to the chemistry student. Then a representative of the police department stopped by to complain that the Dekes were on the loose again; they had gone the rounds of the Main Street barber shops and taken custody of every last cuspidor in town.

By cutting short his noon hour and postponing an appointment with the traveling secretary of Lambda Mu Phi, the dean managed to clean up his morning correspondence, sign the forms for the treasurer's office, skim through the faculty reports, and get to the committee meeting on time with a rough draft of his summary.

Altogether it was a routine morning. That day, like all days, was made up of frustrating interruptions, and it wasn't so much the nagging details that wore him down as the everlasting shifting of emotional gears to accommodate the particular frame of mind brought in by each new patient. Four consecutive visitors could have precisely

the same problem, but all four dressed it in utterly different trimmings, and the dean had to make corresponding
adjustments in his sensibilities. That was the wearing
part.

Threats to life and limb can't be counted on as daily
occurrences in a dean's office, but his routine in the course
of twenty-four hours runs just about the full scale of the
emotions. He is called upon to make spot decisions on
perplexities that a Solomon would prefer to pause over;
everlastingly he is responsible for directing youthful energies that can turn whimsically toward either construction
or destruction; he is in a position to kindle or kill the spark
that may one day alter the course of history.

Collectively, deans of students carry an influence that
affects the destiny of a nation perhaps more than any
other administrative profession, for the talent that is to
solve America's problems of tomorrow comes from the
column of patrons that file in and out of their offices for
counsel and stimulation.

But despite all the responsibility he carries, the dean
is still the most misunderstood character in the academic
procession. To the public he is the campus spoilsport, the
man who orders the vital tackle out of action just before
the big home game, the temperance agitator who has an
overwhelming aversion to bourbon and beer, the stuffy
upholder of standards who ranks English history ahead
of hockey, geology ahead of jazz, philosophy ahead of
fraternity initiations, the symbol of authority against
whom university riots are waged.

ALL THE DEAN'S HORSES AND ALL THE DEAN'S MEN
COULDN'T KEEP U.C. STUDENTS FROM RIOTING AGAIN.[1]

That was the Humpty Dumpty parody headlined in a
San Francisco Bay area daily after an explosive 1957 rally
with forbidden flares, illegal cherry firecrackers and
homemade bombs at the University of California. A few
thousand Berkeley spectators would have been enor-
mously disappointed without the extra excitement, but
the newspapers made it appear that the whole affair was
staged specifically to annoy Dean Hurford Stone, imply-
ing that there would have been no celebration if he
hadn't been personally inept in controlling a student body
of fourteen thousand. For a long time the press and the
practical jokers, Hollywood and the humor magazines,
cartoonists and the comedians have been pouring out
the propaganda until the dean has been popularly reduced to a kill-joy.

That applies, of course, to the official in charge of
student relations. On the college roster is a confusing
menagerie of deans—deans of the faculty; deans of divi-
sions, departments, and schools; deans of admission and
deans of arts and sciences; deans of freshmen; deans of
students, of men, of women, of graduate students. A generation ago, just as deans of men were coming into being,
a University of Oregon reactionary named Edward Thurber shuffled through a shelf of college catalogues and
was appalled at the scourge of deans he found infiltrating
the halls of learning. He foresaw a hierarchy of titled
officials breaking down the democratic traditions. In his
self-imposed position as census taker of deans, he came

across a graduate school dean without any graduate students, a department of journalism with two instructors—one of whom deaned the other—a one-man pedagogy department conducted by a dean of education, and in a really dean-minded college actually a Dean of Deans.

"The last title strikes one as Biblical," he wrote in a constrained summary for the *Nation*, "the others as essentially Miltonic. . . . What, pray, is all this deanerie about? . . . the Dean may be a pleasant fellow, too; he is simply under the shadow of a monstrous name. . . . Would it be imaginable, I wonder, for this snobbery of deans to die a natural, hasty and certain death?"[2]

Thurber's boycott was never very successful, though he did rally a few supporters. Here and there deans were converted into "vice-presidents," "advisers," and "directors." Premature prophecies were made that deans of men and deans of women wouldn't survive. The president of Earlham, for instance, did away with his dean and substituted a presidential assistant with the quip: "So far as I have any feeling in the matter, a rose by any other name would smell as sweet." [3] Ever gullible to new fads and fangles, the world of higher education responded to a new movement that was to put all student relations under "Personnel Directors," and in anticipation of that millennium, a nationwide organization of deans of men, after years of debate, reconstituted themselves under the imposing title "National Association of Student Personnel Administrators."

The abolition movement took its toll, but for every dean that was dropped in one locality, two more bobbed up elsewhere. Someone had to do the superintending and the disciplining, and it wasn't possible to dodge the distasteful chores by hiding behind an untainted title. Instead of diminishing, deans kept multiplying, and in the years since critic Thurber spoke out, instead of losing status, deans of students have become more firmly entrenched than ever, most of them with a supporting retinue of assistants and associates.

All the jockeying for titular recognition is over the heads of undergraduates. The dean is the man they go to when they are in trouble, when they need an advocate, when they have a grievance to air. Regardless of the title in the college catalogue, he is the official from whom the derelict with a bad conscience expects a summons, and with whom the goof knows he will eventually have to reckon. Sometimes the duties of the dean are intricately departmentalized, sometimes he is labeled "Head of Student Relations," "Director of Student Welfare," "of Student Affairs," "Student Life," "Student Activities." Many a dean is convinced that old-fashioned disciplining shouldn't get mixed up with new-style counseling, and a student with symptoms of loose morale or loose morals may be shuffled from office to office, getting a little departmentalized treatment at each, until he is so wearied by the bureaucracy that he decides it is easier to feign normality.

The falderal fools few students. To them the title doesn't matter. They have an instinct for sniffing their way to the proper suite. Dean of Students, Dean of Men, Dean of Women are the most familiar door legends. In the muddle over honorifics, the official to whom students customarily go for their reckonings and advisings is known simply as "the Dean."

"You are requested to report to Dean Gulch's office at 3:15 P.M. on Wednesday" is the most common form of academic subpoena in America, but the offices to which students from Schenectady to San Diego report have little in common physically. Except for the properties, no two stagings are alike. Deans are tucked away in cramped, upper-story cubbyholes; they are lodged in abandoned classrooms—cavernous chambers long ago condemned as firetraps for any other occupants; they are occasionally provided with handsome first-floor apartments as pleasant and accessible as the lounge of the Student Union. There are always at least two rooms—the inner and the outer—with a more or less soundproof door separating the two. His Excellence occupies the inner, the secretary the outer. And the secretary, of course, is the imperious stage director. Surrounded by banks of files containing the secrets of generations of undergraduates, sitting in a confusion of documents, pink slips, cards, and mimeographed forms, she rules supreme.

Sometimes there are rails to guard her official business from straying eyes of inquisitive students; sometimes there is a counter; sometimes a barrier of judiciously placed record cabinets. Between spasms at the typewriter and incessant phone interruptions, she maintains order among the throng of pilgrims who are always waiting on the benches and chairs around the walls. She is the dean's protector and buffer, familiar with most of his confidences and anxieties, keeper of the calendar; she instinctively

37

knows when to tell whom that her superior is "out," is "busy," has a committee meeting that will take most of the afternoon, will be free in "just a minute." She is an efficient boss, imaginative, competent, necessarily domineering. Without her, the office would fold tomorrow. The dean may be an important figure; she is indispensable. When Dean Herbert Hawkes at Columbia caught on to the fact that his secretary was overloaded with student appeals and sometimes too severe in her response, he gallantly revised the seating arrangement so that every undergraduate had to pass his desk in order to see her.

What actually goes on in the different offices varies almost as much as the settings. There is no standard dean of students. It is likely that he has general supervision over the welfare and conduct of students, but beyond that he may be anything from part-time grounds manager to part-time president. He may teach a course or two, may double as chaplain, may boss the faculty, may supervise admissions, registration, and placement services; he may edit the catalogue and make speeches at all the alumni dinners; he may even play father to the girls as well as the boys.

Time was when a co-ed would no more think of presenting herself before a male dean than of barging into the football lockers, and when the captain of the wrestling team was as out of place in the office of the dean of women as in a boudoir. But, to the horror of old grads, these partitions have all broken down. The dean of students in a coeducational institution sees as many women as men and is no more partisan than a general practitioner—though he normally has a dean of men and a dean of women from whom he can seek consolation and to whom he can refer his more inscrutable perplexities. And occasionally a woman holds the top position, as at Reed College in Oregon, where Dean Ann W. Shepard for years competently carried the dual role alone and only recently acquired an associate of the opposite sex.

"He is not, and will not be, Dean of Men," asserts Miss Shepard resolutely, "and I am not, and shall not be, Dean of Women. I should be tremendously disappointed ever to return to what has come to seem a thoroughly artificial, meaningless division of labor. We have learned that who-comes-to-consult-whom can be a matter of student choice or it may be a matter of pure chance. Apparently some men talk more freely with a woman and some women speak more openly to a man—no matter what the topic. Men students have talked with me about almost every-thing: sex, drinking, roommates, money, parents—though I *think* there is an area of reserve about some 'medical' matters. After fifteen years of responsibility as one kind of dean or another, I believe it is *very* important to provide students with an opportunity to choose freely whether they wish to consult a man or a woman, that no coercion should push them toward either counselor, and that since the world is a coeducational business, the world of college should not differ sharply. Much as I enjoy working with people of my own sex, it would seem dull indeed to return to spending my days exclusively with women."

To the protectors of time-tested college conventions, such convictions are rank heresy, and only in the more progressive universities does one find much evidence of the kind of enlightenment Dean Shepard certifies. Nationally there is an accepted—but rarely articulated—policy of aloofness between male and female deans. In round-the-clock harassment and in variety of emotional turmoil encountered, they have much in common, yet the shades of difference in their stewardship can be as subtle as the offices of barber and beautician. Simple generalizations about the art of deaning can seldom be applied to two sexes without half-page footnotes on the deviations and discrepancies. To avoid trouble, most authors treating the supervision of masculine and feminine college students do well to discuss them in separate paragraphs —or, better still, separate volumes.

In the male dean, versatility and adaptability are more essential than a Ph.D. After petitioning the Almighty in Biblical lingo for salvation of his students, he steps down from the pulpit and heads for a suburban beer joint to petition the cops in underworld lingo for student salvation from the grip of local law. He is expected to put on a good performance as a TV educational commentator and an equally good performance as umpire at a raucous interfraternity free-for-all. He sounds off at a committee hearing of the state legislature on the subject of student automobile accidents and the necessity of cars for student transportation, and hurries home to pick up the pieces following another fatal crack-up. He has to be blessed with the patience of a saint and an infallible memory, for his dinners are invariably interrupted by long-distance calls from parents who want to cross-examine him on the reasons for Johnnie's failure in that physics quiz or the economics final.

His reputation for being omniscient and omnipresent is fabulous—though that repute is usually gained more by accident than design. "Boy, am I drunk," bellowed an upperclassman stepping out of his car a little after midnight on sorority row at William and Mary, and obviously out for no good. "Girls, I'm stinko," he whooped, as lights flashed on in the Kappa house. "Save me, Dean! Dean Hocutt, come and get me."

"Did you call, Bill?" came the quiet answer from an apparition not eight feet from the serenader. Dean Hocutt just happened to be out walking off a case of insomnia.

At Norman, Oklahoma, where the administration prided itself in the fine attitude of undergraduates toward the University's integration program, a group of students cruising in their slick convertible one autumn afternoon spotted a racing jalopy driven by a chubby Negro woman who had the impudence to display on her windshield the sacred insignia of their fraternity. To be sure, they knew that the car had recently been sold by one of the brothers, and car owners had repeatedly been admonished to remove decals before making trade-ins. Nevertheless, this was a travesty that had to be set to rights. The convertible gave chase, and immediately the driver of the car in the lead realized that she was being pursued by some unsavory-looking customers. The two cars careened around the University of Oklahoma campus, wove through the congested traffic of Norman, streaked past red lights, and hurtled into the residential section where the quarry took a sudden right into a private drive, leaped out of the car and dashed for a front door. The

41

pursuers skidded to a stop on the front lawn, piled out of the convertible and rushed up the porch steps—where they were calmly greeted by Dean Jodie Smith who, in tempered words, wanted to know why they were rutting his front lawn and chasing his maid.

At any hour of the night the dean's phone rings, summoning him to the police station to commiserate with a student behind bars, or to the hospital to make arrangements for an emergency appendectomy. He has to be particularly adept at subduing riots, like the little one at Carleton College back in 1946 when veterans were returning from the wars to reclaim their co-ed dates, and high school boys, who had been filling in during their absence, bitterly resented the usurpation; or the bigger one at Dartmouth that wasn't broken until Dean Kiendl shinnied up a convenient telegraph pole and harangued his revolutionaries from aloft.

He has to turn deaf ears to unsults not intended for his hearing: "Before those goddamned swindlers from the college arrive, I want to warn you that they are going to try to rook us," Dean Charles Lewis of North Dakota was admonished by an alumnus at a fraternity house where he had been politely invited to help arrange the sale of the house to the University—and hadn't been intelligibly introduced. And at the University of Massachusetts, unrecognized in a darkened dormitory corridor, the dean's representative, Geoffrey Cornish, reached for a light switch just as a freshman prankster pulled a false fire alarm and was familiarly accosted: "Don't turn those lights on, you crazy bastard; you'll have that sonofabitch Cornish up here."

42

Alternately the dean is a sort of pastor and policeman, teacher and tyrant, sympathetic counselor and condemning judge. Too often he is forced into the ambiguous position of representing the whole reach of law enforcement, and, in succession, serves as detective, prosecutor, defendant, jury, and judge for a single infraction.

It happens this way, originating with a Monday-morning phone report from the authorities of a neighboring college: "Say, dean, we're missing a brand-new radio–victrola console from our student union. Disappeared sometime between eleven and midnight last Saturday. . . . Yes, that's right, it was a big party week end here with lots of students from a lot of colleges. The union was jammed solid with the overflow from the fraternities. Funny thing is, we can't find a single witness to the theft. It was a Magnavox; you know what they're like. One man could carry it, but not very inconspicuously, and it's not too easy to hide. With the help of the dormitory counselors, we checked every room. Haven't found a trace. And the only lead we've picked up in our investigations is a frequent reference to a group of young barnstormers from your bailiwick. They didn't have any dates, were pretty rough, and under the influence, I'm told. Now, dean, understand, this is no accusation or anything, but can you give us a hand, just be on the lookout for the console? It represents an investment of several hundred dollars."

A clear case of grand larceny.

The dean takes over as detective. He isn't optimistic about turning up any clues, but this is one of those intercollegiate services he has to perform. Enough casual inquiries are made over a period of two days to convince him that a considerable number of his students were on the prowl that week end, and a delegation of eighteen or twenty Lambda Alphas took advantage of open-house atmosphere at the brother institution. Making off with a souvenir console wouldn't have been out of character with that group.

Meantime, just as he is narrowing down the possible suspects another call comes from the authorities: "Sorry to have bothered you, dean. Forget the whole business. The record player has just been returned. Came in by railway express, intact, unharmed, in perfect working order. Shipped from Clarksville (a little town halfway between the two colleges). Return name and address on the parcel obviously false—almost illegible."

The dean–detective is hesitant about dropping his investigation and letting some misguided culprit continue in his misguided ways—if he can be identified. "Would you," he inquired, "want to send over the wrapping for anything it might reveal?"

"Sure," came the answer, "we'll mail it special delivery, but don't carry this any further on our account. We wanted the machine back, that's all. We're not interested in pressing any charges."

The wrapping arrives at the dean's office. Twenty personnel folders come out of the files and samples of handwriting are checked against the disguised scrawls. Only one man could write his *g*s and *k*s in that peculiar style.

The dean drops his role as detective and turns prosecutor.

The suspect is summoned, and, without any explana-

44

tion, handed the evidence. No prompting is necessary. A confession pours out: the felon had had a lousy time at the party. Yes, he had been drinking too much, and because of it, bouncers kept him from entering any of the fraternity houses. He knew he was noisy—and plenty burned at the lack of hospitality. So he went to the jam-packed student union where everyone—except him—seemed to be having a rousing good time. That made him still more furious. He tried to join little groups, but the only attention he got was a cold shoulder. Intent on retribution, he strolled over to the unattended record-player, closed the lid, unplugged the cord, and carried it out the front door. Even then nobody missed the music or looked his way. He shoved it into the trunk of his car, drove home, and turned in. Next morning he faced the evidence of his foray. He didn't want the damned console, so he rummaged around in the fraternity basement until he found a carton of approximately the right dimensions, cut a class, and took the package all the way to the Clarksville Railway Express office, where he wouldn't be recognized. The shipment cost him a lot of money too.

The prosecutor figuratively dons his judicial robes.

"You realize you could be jailed for this," growls the dean.

"I swear, dean, if you'll take it easy this time, I'll never let you regret it. When I woke up Sunday morning, I knew how serious it was. I got awful mad at myself. It was the liquor that did it. Before I got out of bed I swore to myself I was through drinking as long as I was in college."

The dean had heard this one before. "Not even a beer?" he taunted.

"Not even a beer from now on."

"You know, your drinking is no campus secret," countered the dean. "You can't keep a pledge like that."

"But I will. I'll put it in writing. If you'll let me stay, and I take another drink before I graduate, I'll just come in and check out voluntarily."

The dean handed him a slip of paper. "On your long-range vow," he said, "you'll have to reckon with your own conscience. I'm interested only in the balance of the year, and won't worry about an occasional can of beer. But any report of intoxication and—"

With sweat dripping from his brow, the boy penned his own ruthless sentence, including disciplinary probation. The pledge may have been violated, but the dean never heard of it.

From such converts deans get most of their Christmas cards. The loyal rooters for a successful dean are seldom the faculty, the administration, the trustees, or others who should be most concerned with education of the individual; they are his own students who know all too well some of the difficult decisions he has to make, some of the chances he has taken in placing faith in men who are not used to that kind of confidence.

Occasionally understanding, too, comes from a parent, like the business executive who had previously been fortified with two decades of experience as college textbook salesman and frequent sessions with deans. When his own son—a freshman with more enthusiasm for football than chemistry—hinted that an appropriate word from home, addressed to the dean, might get him out of looming difficulties, the father was ready.

"You know that you can always count on us for backing," he wrote his son, "but when someone else is better equipped to give you assistance, I'm not going to interfere. The Dean's your man. Occasionally there are duds in dean's offices, but not very often, for they don't last long, and you don't have that kind. The best advice I can give you is to make yourself known to the Dean before there's a crisis. Don't try to soft-soap him, put anything over on him, con him for favors and concessions. He's all too familiar with that approach, and polite enough to let the insult pass without acknowledging it. He's a very busy man, but he has time to listen to anyone with honest intentions. Once you have impressed him with what you're aiming at, he will be your best ally when you need one. In choosing a college you also chose him. Subject to his counsel, you're on your own. It's got to be pretty much your party from now on. You owe it to yourself to do the engineering. You wouldn't want me to intercede. My butting in would be as out of place as rushing onto the field to tell off the referee when he had called you for a disputed offside. The Dean's a good coach. If you can improve the score, you should convince him you can do it. Talk it over with him. You'll never regret it."

Father was right. If parents would only permit sons to settle their own doubts at the right desk, if detractors in Hollywood, on Madison Avenue, and in alumni circles would lay off for a few years, the dean might turn into a very satisfactory American champion.

2.

"NOT TO KNOW THE DEAN
IS A CERTIFICATE
OF GOOD CHARACTER"

[The President as Dean]

THE DEAN as a counselor, guardian, and apologist for undergraduates was an American creation. Oxford and Cambridge both employed husky tyrants whose principal task was to round up and flog errant scholars, "certain censors or *deanes*, appointed to look to the behavior and manner of the Students, whom they punish very severely, if they make any default, according to the quantitye and qualitye of their trespasses." [1] In medieval monasteries deans imposed an uncompromising regimen upon the young monks placed under their supervision; in the Anglican cathedral, they held similar sway over a chapter of canons; long before that there was a military dean, *decanus*, a sort of sergeant who barked orders to subalterns.

But on this side of the Atlantic, ivy had been spreading over the walls of colleges for more than two centuries before deans were considered essential to academic order. Here and there heads of quasi-independent medical

schools in search of university patronage called themselves deans instead of presidents, but to undergraduates the title was virtually unknown. Until the last decades of the 1800s, American students were spared the
tyranny of the dean's office.

During that long reprieve, however, undergraduates
were not exempt from the authoritative chastening customarily provided by proctors, censors, and "deanes" in
brother institutions abroad. College presidents themselves ably filled the gap, wielded the rod, laid down the
law, and set a formidable standard of enforcement procedure—with occasional support from muscular proctors
and classics professors. So callous and so durable was the
standard set by these masters of chastisement that deans
to this day have not succeeded entirely in shaking off
their influence.

Almost without exception early educational executives
were gospel ministers. Their pastorate was a college community and the pastoral duties among undergraduates
merely an adaptation of the pastoral duties performed in
a village. They offered wise counsel, both spiritual and
material, to individual students, taught the more erudite
phases of philosophy and theology, and in daily chapel
services expounded on the advantages of a virtuous life.
But they soon discovered that it took more than pulpit
exhortation to prod a youthful audience along the paths
of righteousness. More forceful measures than exhortation were called for. One had to scour the waterfront of a
seaport to find a more troublesome lot. Individually, the
teen-agers who composed a college congregation could
be as innocent and guileless as their sisters; collectively

they could act like an organized deputation from the abode of the damned. They swore, they gambled, they drank, they chased women, they took the name of the Lord in vain—and worse still, they neglected their studies. Admonition failed to yield anything more than temporary reform.

In civil life the pillory and the local prison helped to make an impression on such culprits, but neither stocks nor irons seemed appropriate to the academic scene. Corporal punishment was still the accepted expedient for bringing undergraduate transgressors to terms, so the president became an expert in flagellation as well as education. A lash was kept at arm's reach in the executive office, and when the leather wasn't handy, many a student crept away from his suppressor bearing on his face untidy swellings that roughly matched the presidential knuckles.

Massachusetts in 1656 spelled out the legal limits to which Harvard could carry her corporal punishment: "It is hereby ordered that the President and Fellows . . . are empowered, according to their best discretion to punish all misdemeanors of the youth in their society either by fine, or whipping in the Hall openly, as the nature of the offence shall require, not exceeding ten shillings or ten stripes for one offence; and this law to continue in force until this Cort or the Overseers of the College provide some other order to punish such offences."[2]

Neither the Massachusetts Court nor the overseers were in too much of a hurry to find substitute legislation, for twenty years later Thomas Sargeant, accused of "speaking blasphemous words concerning the Holy Ghost," was hauled in for a public whipping. For this occasion the student body was formally assembled in the library. The sentence was solemnly read, a prayer in behalf of Thomas offered by the President, the stripes were applied, and then the whole ceremony appropriately capped with a sacred benediction.

At Yale "boxing" or "cuffing" an offender was preferred, and there the practice went on until 1755. By virtue of his office the president was the privileged assailant, though the faculty rather than the student body were normally assembled to bear witness "while blows fell in quick succession upon either ear." But dignity was lost on one occasion when a particularly notorious second offender was brought to account. The faculty had taken their ringside seats; the culprit entered sulkily and stood before them, assuming the proper angle with bowed head ready for the stunning blows. The President finished his summary of misdeeds and advanced upon the sophomore. He swung a right and missed. The accused, not fully in sympathy with this means of redemption, was ready to demonstrate that he could dodge blows as dextrously as the President could apply them. The executive tried a left and failed to make contact. With rising indignation he charged forward with a bruising haymaker, but the sophomore was not there to receive it. Nimbly he had stepped aside, and saved the President further embarrassment by hightailing it out of the room—and out of college.

To prove their worth as educators, it was essential that the presidents, the fellows, and faculty demonstrate to the public that they could keep the boys at their books, mold character, and control the carousing. They were ingenious at discovering new punitive measures and new forms of humiliation. The high purpose of the disciplinarians was to make such a memorable example in the treatment of a miscreant, that his fellow students would shrink from temptation; and, if at all possible, he had to be kept on the college rolls where he could suffer for his sins and be seen to suffer. The sentence of permanent expulsion was issued only as a last resort, for it was an admission of defeat on the part of the authorities. Suspension or rustication was tried first; the troublemaker was farmed out for a cooling-off period of a week or term on the chance that some of the prudence of a minister or husbandman, to whom he was paroled, would rub off on him. In any of the New England towns legal banishment from a community was a sinister punishment, and its application to college society was a threat fully as grave.

But remaining in residence under some of the conditions imposed by the president was not much more attractive than banishment. A miscreant could be confined to his quarters, required to sit conspicuously alone and hatless in commons, ordered to recite a detailed confession of his crime before the student body. He could be given "impositions," which meant doing endless exercises in copying from a dry sermon or, worse, committing it to memory. Pilferage, intoxication, or destruction of property could bring on the penalty of "deduction"—a lowering of every grade earned in class work. And anything as serious as swearing or blasphemy brought "degradation," the most ignominious treatment that could be conferred upon a student with respectable family background.

Instead of neat alphabetical arrangements, all class

rolls were prepared in order of parental rank, and degradation involved automatic displacement in that rank. Aristocrats, boys who could boast of noble British sires, sons of magistrates, clergymen, and professional men, headed the list, and the order determined the social position of every student, the listing of names in the catalogue, the seating in chapel, the line-up of the Commencement procession. No punishment could be more disgraceful for the heir of a councilman than to be forced to give up his front seat in chapel and sit beside the shoemaker's boy in the back row.

A tutor brings in three Harvard students caught in the act of robbing a hen coop and the record goes on the blotter for all time: "November 4th, 1717. Three scholars were publicly admonished for thievery, and one degraded below five in his class, because he had been before publicly admonished for card-playing. They were ordered by the President into the middle of the Hall (while two others, concealers of the theft, were ordered to stand up in their places, and spoken to there). The crime they were charged with was first declared, and then laid open as against the law of God and the House, and they were admonished to consider the nature and tendency of it, with its aggravations; and all, with them, were warned to take heed and regulate themselves . . . lest God tear them in pieces, according to the text. They were then fined, and ordered to make restitution twofold for each theft."[3]

Determining the precedence of students for the class roll was the most delicate task a president had to perform, for no matter how diplomatically it was drawn up, he could count on a parade of insulted parents storming his office for reconsideration. In 1768 Yale, "embued with the notion of equality," made a radical and unpopular departure from the old tradition by listing all students alphabetically. Abolishment of rank came harder for the Boston clientele, but Harvard followed suit five years later. The presidents were relieved of a distasteful chore, but they also forfeited the most effective disciplinary measure ever dreamed up by educational administrators.

The president, as disciplinarian, literally held the big stick over his charges in those early years. He was required to spend less time on the road in search of endowment funds and could afford to devote some of his energies to problems of student personnel. Penology was as important to him as theology. Punishment was calculated to be justified whether or not it might lead constructively to more acceptable behavior and the rehabilitation of an offender. And he was very, very slow to catch on that his system didn't work. Tough as his penalties were, they didn't bring order to the yard. As fast as he could think up new regulations, his students thought up new ways of violating them. Alcoholic indulgence, pyrotechnics, plagiarism, overcutting, profanity, petty thievery continued to be tribulations of his office. And as colleges spread over other parts of the country the situation was not very different; the disciplinarians were incessantly tormented by student crimes and misdemeanors committed in the guise of sport.

Way down east in rural Brunswick, Bowdoin collegians annually staged their "hold-ins," when the sophomores precipitated a free-for-all by barricading the freshmen in chapel after evening prayers; annually "Yager fights" were stirred up to assault the gangs of lumbermen coming down the river in the spring; annually they upset the town and the faculty with spectacular conflagrations— raising a seventy-foot pole, stacking around it tar-drenched barrels and brush, and touching it off.

Hamilton refined the bonfire idea with an annual November "Joe-burning," when the president or some other unpopular dignitary in the community could expect to find himself without sanitary facilities in his back yard. On a monumental pyramid of pilfered fence rails, logs, and lumber, the appropriated "Joes" were mounted, filled with tar-soaked straw, and set afire in a glorious blaze that could be seen for twenty miles. The faculty bustled about, officiously executing the President's commands, making a show of rescuing a particularly pretentious privy, trying to restore order and identify ringleaders, but it was hopeless. On this mad night once a year all control of the college was lost. In grotesque masquerade, the students dashed about the campus on horseback to the terror and delight of the townsfolk, and toward daybreak when the authorities had given up the chase, all joined hands in a pagan ritual around the dying fire to chant a Latin dirge dedicated to Joseph: *Ponamus convivium / Joseph in locum / Et id uremus.*

Far to the south, the President of the College of South Carolina had much the same problem to contend with. There it was "black riding"—a high offense punishable by expulsion. But rarely could college law catch up with the black-face masqueraders shrouded in hideous hoods, and making a God-awful disturbance with horns and shouting. On horseback they raced back and forth across the hallowed yard, always outdistancing the proctors who rode almost as hard in pursuit.

Periodic orgies of hornblowing were the anathema of all guardians of college law and order—a pandemonium calculated to sound as though heaven had fallen, hell had broken loose, and the two were in violent conflict. Inevitably it brought all local and academic law enforcement agents on the run. At Princeton the entire student body, armed with horns, bugles, and trumpets on a prearranged midnight, distributed itself in the tops of trees, and at a signal gave forth. The bedlam was exquisitely timed to last just long enough to accomplish its effect, and when the authorities bore down, the noisemakers were innocently under the covers. Woe unto him who was slow in his retreat from a treetop. Many a Princetonian was obliged to spend the cold morning hours aloft, hiding in the foliage, waiting for the all-clear.

At Dartmouth students turned out en masse in 1851 to help celebrate the arrival of the first locomotive at White River Junction. Appropriate to the occasion, they carried with them their horns and bottles, and were so incensed when chastised for interrupting speeches that they opened up with a barrage of noise that lasted for hours. Eleven malefactors were dismissed, and a statute prohibiting hornblowing went on the books. But statutes did not silence the tooters. The racket continued for forty-five years, until in 1896 students themselves were a little wearied of it and consented to abandon the custom.

To punctuate the cacophony of brass and tin, firearms and cannon were frequently brought into play. Citizens of Hanover assumed that an earthquake had shaken the region one rainy night in 1834 until they learned the next morning that a cannon fired outside the room of an unpopular student had shattered 120 panes of glass in the hall. But the disciplinarians ingeniously caught up with that one. Sharply-molded boot tracks were observed around the site of the field piece, and during the small hours of the morning, the faculty went the rounds of the sleeping quarters looking for wet boots to match the tracks. In the process, helpful student volunteers succeeded in obliterating most of the evidence, so that only one boot track was definitely matched. The owner of that boot bade farewell to the hills of New Hampshire.

Not to be outdone by Dartmouth, the scholarly lads at Hamilton dragged a cannon to the top floor of a dormitory, heavily charged and fired it point-blank at the door of an insufferable captive tutor.

The standard response to an unpalatable edict from the president was a strike or riot. In some colleges the uprisings came almost as regularly as spring thaw or winter solstice—riots over unsavory food at the commons, riots in protest of the dismissal of a student, library riots, chapel riots, commencement riots, riots staged for no conceivable cause except the urgent need for a break in college routine.

Yale, Harvard, and Princeton set the examples in colorful demonstrations for younger institutions to emulate—and they were merely following well-known precedents established at Oxford where over fifty students and townsmen died in the battle of St. Scholastica's Day in 1355, or at Cambridge where the High Steward is still appointed annually to attend the hanging of undergraduates who indulge in such massacres. The American rebellions were mild by comparison, usually set off by some minor incident or minor official, like the commons steward at Harvard who allegedly served butter so rancid that "a farmer would not take it to grease his cartwheels with," and mutton stew dished out with such regularity that after a six weeks' daily diet of it the diners once assembled en masse in the steward's front yard, and "as if their natures had been changed by the diet, would bleat and blatter until he was fain to promise them a change." Finally the trustees agreed that "the disturbances were not wholly without cause," and after listening to complaints about rancid butter and mutton stew for two centuries they closed the commons.[4]

Harvard commencements rivaled the festivities of a county fair. "The Common was covered with booths erected in lines like streets," wrote one historian. "In these booths were carried on all sorts of dissipation. Here was a knot of gamblers, gathered around a wheel of fortune, or watching the whirl of a ball on a roulette-table. Farther along, the jolly hucksters displayed their tempting wares in the shape of cooling beverages and palate-tickling confections. There was dancing on this side, auction-selling on the other; here a pantomimic show, there a blind man, led by a dog, soliciting alms; organ-grinders and hurdy-gurdy grinders, bears, and monkeys, jugglers and sword-swallowers, all mingled in inextricable confusion. . . . Nor was there any want of the spirituous; pails of punch, guarded by stout negroes, bore witness to their own subtle contents, now by the man who lay curled up under the adjoining hedge, forgetting and forgot, and

again the drunkard, reeling, cursing and fighting among his comrades."

"Pyramids of Egypt! can ye surpass these enormous piles?" exclaimed another witness on first sighting the college buildings in commencement array. "The common covered with tents and wigwams, and people of all sorts, colors, conditions, nations, and tongues. A country muster or ordination dwindles into nothing in comparison. It was a second edition of Babel."

All that the setting needed for climax was a student riot on Commencement Day and the graduating class all too willingly supplied it. One year it would be provoked by a proctor trying to enforce the regulation against setups of "meat and drinks" in the rooms; the next by the graduating class squabbling over who was to serve as marshal: "The partisans fell on each other pell-mell; scarce heeding in their hot affray the orders of the Faculty, the threats of the constables, or the rebuke of the chief magistrate of the State; the alumni were left to find their seats in the church as best they could, the aged and beloved President following in sorrow, unescorted, to perform the duties of the day." [5]

The clamor went on periodically through the 1700s and well into the 1800s without respect for venerable officials, faculty members or omniscient proctors. In rural colleges presidents arrived at the chapel for morning services to find geese, goats, and cattle tethered to their pulpits in token disapproval of the oratory delivered there, and a word from an upperclassman was sufficient to turn the hilarity that followed into a twenty-four-hour mutiny.

While one conscientious mob of students at Dartmouth

was whooping up a tar-and-feather attack to express their indignation over the male keeper of a house of ill-fame, a few select dissenters were being entertained in their rooms by the naked dancing of the keeper's daughter. There was no consistency.

At Princeton in 1807 the entire student body rose up in defense of three students who had been ignobly dismissed for drunkenness, profanity, and insubordination. Since it was impossible to cope with the insurgents by more subtle means, the college closed its doors until tempers had cooled. And on a sabbath morning ten years later, an angry throng of students locked several tutors into their rooms and set fire to the building. Again the rioters were ordered to evacuate the college, but this time they staged a sit-down, refused to budge from their rooms. It took the combined efforts of the President, the Trustees, the local police, and the faculty to oust a dozen men. Nassau Hall, a national shrine where the Continental Congress had met for six months in 1783, was irreverently blown up with dynamite three times by rioting Princetonians.

The presidents who were trying to administer discipline to these generations of undergraduates were distinguished clergymen, philosophers, scholars, teachers, authors, but they were doing a most undistinguished job of deaning—and their entourage of tutors, proctors, and faculty elders was not doing much better. The approach was dictatorial and vindictive. They had to demonstrate their authority. It was beneath their dignity to solicit student cooperation. They couldn't catch on to the fact that sophomoric upstarts above all craved attention, loved nothing more than to lead a merry chase, and as long as the energy of the pursuers held out, the boys would keep a few jumps ahead. The oldsters didn't realize that forbearance in overlooking the pranks and in making light of minor infractions would have forestalled the crescendo of more serious lawlessness. The only psychology they knew and practiced was as old as the Old Testament. There had to be a law and a penalty to meet every situation. The idea of student participation in maintaining order hadn't yet been born.

In a real crisis, rather than rely on their own wisdom and run the risk of trustee disapproval, the presidents called upon the corporation for a solution—and that surrender of authority could only be interpreted by students as an admission of incompetence. Moreover, the dictum of the board almost invariably proved to be tactless and unrealistic. Many of the presidents were in such a precarious spot that they had to take refuge in protective laws created especially for them: "If any scholar shall assault, wound, or strike the President, or shall maliciously and designedly break his windows or doors, he shall be expelled."

The law wasn't enough. Presidents and professors continued to live in mortal terror of the youth they were guiding. With a crust of stale bread, a Harvard student scored a hit on the left eye of historian William Prescott and blinded the eye. University of Virginia faculty members were subjected to brutal assaults, and in 1842 a professor there was shot and killed by a trigger-happy assailant. At Oakland College in Mississippi a drunken student satisfied his grudge against the President by stabbing him to death. Dignified men of letters were stoned, whipped, and ridden out of town.

Between diversions, juvenile delinquents were well disciplined in subjects like ancient languages, mathematics, natural philosophy, and Biblical chronology. Boys with a seriousness of purpose received good counsel and a good education, and probably they were a majority, but they received it from martinets in an atmosphere of distrust, compulsion, and disorder.

When the first deans began to take over as student guardians in the late 1800s and early 1900s, they already had two outs and two strikes against them. They were being handed a thankless job in which more experienced men had failed, a responsibility that nobody wanted very much. With it went the long, colorful record of methods used unsuccessfully to promote acceptable standards of conduct and scholarly endeavor: they were expected to use the same methods successfully. The situation as described at the University of Illinois in 1901, just before the first Dean of Men received his appointment, was fairly representative of the *esprit de corps* on other campuses: "The faculty paid little, if any, attention to the students outside class hours. The students came and went as they pleased. Their discipline was so poor that they practically drove away the two previous regents, who could not cope with their pranks, practical jokes, and fun." [6]

Not that affairs would have been in a better state if there had been deans from the beginning. The authoritarian climate would have precluded it. The real trouble was that too many duties had been heaped upon the president. As his institution grew, he had to spend an increasing amount of time as an itinerant begging for funds. The accumulation of student and alumni records, the broadening college interests, and the formidable correspondence necessary for maintaining amiable public relations were turning him into a bureaucrat. He had to relinquish much of his teaching load, accept fewer outside pulpit engagements; and more and more he had to slight his pastoral duties with students. Giant of a man though he was, he could not survive under the weight of responsibilities as registrar, financier, admissions director, alumni secretary, and dean.

His first relief usually came with the appointment of a business manager. Various chores were parceled out to faculty committees. The president's secretary often took care of what counseling was done. An "excusing officer" was designated for each class, charged with outflanking the battery of students who had been bombarding the president with reasons for not attending chapel and classes. Then in 1870 Harvard's new president, Charles W. Eliot, came up with the most novel proposal of all: he called for an assistant to be labeled "Dean of the College." It was a scandalous whim for a college president to consider yielding to another what had long been regarded as his chief reason for being. But a subordinate to supervise the curriculum was what Dr. Eliot wanted, and what his corporation reluctantly agreed to—a radical alteration in the whole educational structure. Professor Ephraim Gurney of the history department took over the post, against the mutterings of his colleagues. His assignment was to look after the welfare of students as well as the long-range interests of instruction.

"Not to Know the Dean Is a Certificate of Good Character"

Even before the appointment of the new Harvard dean, however, at most colleges a few faculty members without executive portfolio had been taking an interest in the "welfare of students," and gradually they received titular recognition. Three thousand miles from the Hub, for instance, at the University of Oregon, Professor John Straub in 1878 unofficially assumed the duties of "dean," and at Johns Hopkins a "chief of advisers" appointed in 1889 to supervise faculty counselors was nicknamed "dean." Elsewhere young professors or excusing officers were voluntarily performing similar duties. During the First World War the title "Dean of Men" was hung on a score of college officers, mostly in the Middle West. But not until the 1920s—the decade that gave birth to a rash of deans from coast to coast—did the title become a conventional fixture.

Meantime, Harvard's Dean of the College had become so successful and so overworked that in 1890 his responsibilities were divided two ways: Gurney's old office was renamed "Deanship of the Faculty of Arts and Science," and to take care of student relations, a popular English professor, LeBaron Russell Briggs, was appointed Dean of Harvard College. Cambridge at the time was sheltering the largest university in the country and, with its controversial elective system, was setting the nation's educational standards. Briggs was to become the exemplary dean of students for a generation, and Harvard's division of administration copied wherever an harassed president held office.

But Harvard is not entitled to all the credit. Actually, women educators for almost a century had been plotting a course for undergraduate guidance that the men's colleges had been largely ignoring. Girls had experienced the advantage of expert supervision ever since female seminaries were first opened, and accordingly had been spared the disrepute acquired by their brothers at Princeton, Dartmouth, and Yale.

Cheerfully bearing such titles as warden, preceptress, matron, and lady principal, guidance officers in the seminaries had proved their competence to accomplish what the presidents had failed to do. They had no insurmountable problems of discipline and anti-intellectualism. Though girls too often quit college after an experimental year or two, invariably they were kept in line as long as they were enrolled.

Then having ably shown that they had the capacity to absorb higher mathematics and Platonic philosophy, they wanted to know why they couldn't sit in on classes with the boys. It was a case of women having an inch and wanting a yard. Was there no limit to their audacity? Everywhere the exponents of coeducation were greeted with indignation. "Women," harangued a respected educator, "are no more capable of enduring the same severe and protracted study with the other sex, by day and by night, through all the months and years of their early life, than they are able to perform the same labors on the farm or in the shop, in the mine or at the anvil, or to brave the same dangers and bear the same hardships and exposures on the tented field. This fact alone goes far to settle the question of coeducation. Sooner or later, in the long run, coeducation will, for this reason alone, inevitably either break down the health and constitution of women, or

66

change the curriculum and lower the standard of college education." [7]

Nevertheless, when the doors of Oberlin were first opened in 1833, the trustees decided to brave the storm of protest and leave at least a side entrance for women. The female intruders were placed under the supervision of a "judicious Lady Principal" charged with correcting their habits and molding the female character. She regulated the social life in the dormitory, was the ultimate authority on all women's problems, was responsible for their discipline. In effect she was the dean of women, more than half a century before there was an official dean of men. The pattern set at Oberlin was followed closely by other colleges bold enough to admit women, and when deans of students were finally introduced to men's colleges they were the legatees of an established tradition. They couldn't deny it; women had done the real pioneering.

Deans of men on a national scale were undoubtedly a by-product of World War I, but long before 1919 the title "Dean of Women" had found a place of respect in college catalogues. These successors of the lady principals had so clearly defined what was expected of a dean of students that rarely did the president or the trustees bother to specify his duties. An exception was at the University of Tennessee where the first dean of men, upon his appointment, was provided with the forthright charge:

"The Dean of Men is a University officer responsible to the central administration, from which he derives his status and authority. He is ex-officio a member of all

67

faculties and of committees which deal with student affairs, delinquencies in studies and disciplinary measures. . . . He has supervision of the welfare of all men students of the University. He has frequent personal interviews with them, advises them in their University life and corresponds with their parents on matters of their conduct. He has oversight of matters concerning both housing and fraternities; he inspects these houses and, in cooperation with the authorities, he approves or disapproves their houses, and sees that proper discipline is maintained in them. He does all in his power among students and faculty to promote a spirit of mutual understanding and good will." [8]

Though presidents elsewhere were singularly sketchy in outlining the dimensions of the job, Tennessee had aptly covered for them.

New plaques were affixed to the doors of abandoned classrooms and makeshift offices. The dreadful day of the dean had come in. Burdened with the encumbrance of tradition bequeathed him by presidents, proctors, excusing officers, faculty advisers, and lady principals, he had a long uphill pull ahead of him. Self-respecting students had always avoided the law enforcement officer, and it did not take long for the new dictum to spread through the college world: "Not to know the dean is a certificate of good character." [9]

3.

"WE GUARANTEE SATISFACTION OR WE RETURN THE BOY"

[The Dean as Guardian]

IN EUROPEAN UNIVERSITIES students shift for themselves with a minimum of supervision. Theirs is a restricted educational system devised for the minority, for qualified intellectuals and the aristocracy on a take-it-or-leave-it basis. Peace officers of one sort or another bear down on those who violate the laws of the land or of the college, but personal academic progress is strictly a private matter. There is no prodding or prompting from professional counselors and psychological guides. In fact, Japan is the only foreign nation in the world that has made much progress in offering such personnel services; countries like Italy, West Germany, Holland, and Belgium are just beginning to recognize the possible need for them. By American standards, the European program of self-reliance is inefficient and inexpensive; it has also been very effective.

Of necessity, the Yankees back in colonial days introduced a different tack. Out of deference to democracy, they abandoned the notion that college training was primarily for the genteel, for the cultured, or even the scholarly. Fathers of peasant ancestry envisioned their sons as magistrates and governors: opportunity was for everyone. Under this revolutionary concept, the high purpose of higher education as it had been known in the mother countries was slowly undermined by the infiltration of the inelegant and the uncouth, by boys more interested in adventure than in becoming gentlemen, by unwilling sons impressed into scholarship by ambitious parents. The lack of enthusiasm for erudition became increasingly infectious during the nineteenth century. It was this infection that presidents had such a rough time in checking and that finally called for the ministration of a specialist called a "dean."

The new officer came on the wave of reaction against the cold scholarly authoritarianism which American Ph.D.s were bringing back with them from their studies in Germany. Democracy demanded more of the humanitarian approach. European psychology of education didn't seem to be catching on in America; nor did the overbearing tyrant of a scholar command the respect he was accorded on the other side of the Atlantic. He was out of character here, and resistance to the kind of discipline he stood for was slowly leading to chaos.

The situation at the University of Illinois was fairly representative of what was occurring nationally about 1900. The President there was at his wits' end trying to cope with problems of discipline and problems of anti-intellectualism. His troubles were epitomized in the case of an undistinguished son of a distinguished state celebrity. Truth was, the President didn't dare fire Fred Applegate; the father had too many connections, and the consequences of dismissing the son would be even more unpleasant than his unwelcome presence on the campus. The obstinate youngster had openly violated every rule on the university books and made remarkable headway with local statutes. He had been in and out of Urbana police courts, and in and out of the President's office. He knew the more odious sections of the city intimately, hobnobbed with the local riffraff, gambled, drank freely, led other students astray, occasionally attended classes but rarely demonstrated any acquaintance with the subject under discussion. There was no excuse for his being allowed to remain in college—aside from the desirability of avoiding the inevitable clash with his father if the young rascal were kicked out.

Fred was due back in the President's office following his latest immoral escapade, and in desperation the executive called for assistance from a thirty-nine-year-old English instructor, Thomas Arkle Clark, who for several years had been exhibiting considerable ingenuity in getting the best out of college misfits, even though his slight, homely figure possessed few of the attributes one associated with a student idol.

As Clark entered the office he could feel the tension. The student and the President sat at opposite sides of the big desk glaring at each other in heavy silence. Both had said all there was to say. Fred had no intention of agreeing to the President's program of reform and the President had obviously issued his last ultimatum.

"Mr. Clark," announced the executive, ignoring the

presence of his problem child, "I don't know what to do with this boy. His grades and his actions are a disgrace to the University. He won't study and he won't go straight. I don't want to dismiss him. I've done the best I could with him and I've failed. I am going to turn him over to you."

"Why pick on me?" inquired the instructor facetiously without giving a hint of his real alarm. This case of scandalous conduct was the gossip of the faculty, and getting involved was the last thing he wanted.

The President left Clark's query hanging in the air and turned to Fred with his final words: "I am giving Mr. Clark an absolutely free rein with you. You are to do whatever he says. If he dismisses you from college, I will back him up."

Clark was not flattered by his new trust. He had the feeling that he had been decorated ingloriously with a millstone. His interest was teaching English; he had come up the hard way. The son of an immigrant coal miner, he had wanted to be a doctor, but the death of his mother and a series of other misfortunes precluded that. He had spent most of his youth plowing, planting, cultivating, and harvesting a 120-acre farm by himself. He had taught district school for a while and hadn't been possessed of the urge to enter college until he was twenty-four. In teaching English, following his graduation, he had belatedly found his calling, and he didn't want to be encumbered with the task of nursing derelicts.

Fred and the English instructor left the office with one thing in common: a hearty aversion for the President's edict. "Let's go get a soda and talk it over," Clark mumbled to his charge as they entered the corridor.

At the fountain the common embarrassment turned into amusement. Both recognized the other's predicament. They stared at each other and laughed. Clark frankly acknowledged that he didn't know how to tackle the assignment; he couldn't bring about a reformation unless the participant was ready to help himself. He discovered that Fred never had done anything constructive of his own accord. His few accomplishments had been all carried out under duress. He had been controlled, nagged, and forced—pulled one way by his father and another by his mother. His father had sent him to college, but his mother came along to provide the necessary supervision. That hadn't worked out. While his mother gullibly believed he was at the library or at chapel exercises, he was cavorting with the dregs of the town. To his newly appointed curator from the English department, Fred openly bragged of his sordid adventures, but behind all the bravado, Clark saw a boy who wasn't nearly as sinister as he tried to be. Given time, he might respond to a kind of treatment different from anything he had ever known.

"Don't expect any demands from me," Clark told him. "Never will I tell you what you can or can't do, where you must or mustn't go. I'm not going to stand in the way of your doing anything you're bent on, but I ask one favor of you: will you keep me honestly informed of your comings and goings? No secrets."

Fred thought that was a small price to pay for freedom of movement and shook hands in agreement.

In the first days of the experiment the unsophisticated Clark learned a great deal he had never known before about police courts, women, saloons, and disreputable sections of town. He listened to the reports and offered no word of chastisement—much to the mixed disappointment and delight of his charge. Neither was quite ready to admit that he was testing the endurance of the other.

"You're the funniest man I ever met," Fred finally acknowledged. "You really mean it about not following me around and prying into my affairs. And you want to continue with it—letting me go my way? My parents, and I'm sure the President, wouldn't approve. No lecturing. No snooping. No threats. I'm not used to your kind of treatment, but I like it."

Confident that Fred was capable of carrying out his own self-analysis and self-restoration, if his observer continued patiently to show the right kind of friendly interest, Clark assured his parolee that he had every intention of keeping his original promise; and the boy at last began to understand. After that, things went more easily for both of them. The English instructor won the endurance test. It was the beginning of a new life for Fred and the end of an old one. Suddenly he made a complete break with his former associates, started studying and getting respectable grades. He took an interest in college affairs, developed a new circle of friends, and proudly included his guardian among them.

Fred was graduated with his class, and on the strength of what his guardian's technique had accomplished, Thomas Arkle Clark became the first dean of the University of Illinois. The year was 1901.

To Dean Clark the new job had one avowed purpose: helping to develop character. "Every man is a case by himself," he explained. "I would not think of laying down rules to be adhered to rigidly under all circumstances. What could be a real punishment for one, might be to the other a challenge to further misdeeds. Every boy can be managed, I'm convinced of that, but every boy can't be fitted into the particular mold you may want to put him into, if it happens to be the wrong mold. A man can be sorry for ten minutes. That leaves no mark. Character is developed by doing things difficult enough to cut lines in a man's soul." [1]

The dean took a grip on the undergraduates at Illinois such as no man in the history of the University had ever done. "He is respected, loved, and sought by students," observed an admirer, "because of mysterious qualities of sympathy and knowledge of human nature which enable him to help them when they feel that their problems are becoming too stiff for them." He kept a ten-hour office day, and the chairs in the waiting room were always full. On an average day he talked to fifty students—fifteen hundred conferences a month, ten thousand a year, and 95 per cent of his protégés came not because they were summoned, but because they wanted to talk to "Tommy Arkle."

In the half-century since the English instructor rescued his first profligate, deans of students or their equivalent have become such stable fixtures on the college staff that it is difficult now to realize that there were once beginners in the field—beginners who were feeling their way into a new profession, establishing a service virtually unknown in other lands, making decisions that were to affect millions of undergraduates for generations to come.

And their tentative efforts were carried on against resistance from all sides. Students, cherishing the old freedoms of college life, resented the intrusion of a watchdog. Faculty members, particularly in smaller colleges, saw no reason why a president of average competence shouldn't be able to control rambunctious students and give them all the advice they needed, without further administrative reinforcements. Presidents themselves— the ones who were most eager to shake off an onerous burden—were not quite sure how much authority they dared surrender to a subordinate, and invariably retained veto power to apply when expedient, regardless of how sorely the dean might be humiliated and discredited in the process. Trustees questioned the advisability of promoting all this paternalism; even parents, who felt it was their privilege to deal directly with the head of the institution, were nettled over being shunted off to a mere dean.

Then in a few colleges there were very unfortunate choices for the post. Short-sighted presidents were inclined to pick strong-arms from the faculty, men who would take their police duties so conscientiously that a memorable example would be set in the punishment of each recalcitrant, men who would smoke out the campus rebels and ride herd on them. They were functionaries far more interested in making their constituency conform to a rigorous code of behavior than in Dean Clark's conception of character structure. Elaborate systems of spies, counterspies, and stool pigeons were set up—with or without compensation. No undergraduate was safe from the pursuit of this predatory official. He was perpetuating the vindictive approach to the mastery of a student body that presidential martinets had been employing since 1638.

"We Guarantee Satisfaction or We Return the Boy"

Under his regime the boy who misjudged the impact of a snowball against a classroom window suffered public admonishment that only inspired him to manufacture harder, speedier, more elusive snowballs. A dispirited junior quietly flunked out, since the dean had no way of gaining his confidence to learn that the reason for a waning interest in embryology and quantitative analysis was a paternal mandate that the son give up his expensive ambition to become a doctor and make plans to take over the family shoe store—a stalemate that might have been forestalled with tactful intercession and counseling. One efficient shepherd of students chose the dinner hour for his more clandestine inspection tours: tipped off by informants that the college newspaper was to come out with a scurrilous editorial about him, he commandeered and destroyed the entire edition before the students left commons; then he summarily banned the paper and sacked the editorial staff. He was working *against* a mass of students rather than *with* or *for* them.

Possibly these taskmasters were a minority among the pioneer deans. They made an indelible impression that survived over the years; in fact, a few of their heirs still exist. But the Tommy Arkles also made an impression. Working quietly and understandingly with the throng of undergraduates who were everlastingly trooping in for advice, they set a standard in student relations which would be remembered long after the martinets were retired or buried. Their idea was that they were guardians taking over where parents left off—or where parents had failed. They filled the gap. They realized the inability of fathers and mothers to accept the truth that by the time a son goes off to college, the parents had done just about all they are going to do in shaping his moral and ethical standards. True, they could add polish, perhaps furnish further incentive, and provide the wherewithal for letting him expand, but, for better or for worse, they had given their seventeen-year-old all the fundamental home indoctrination he was likely to absorb from them. If it were otherwise, something was wrong. Into the first seventeen years the parents were allowed the opportunity to pack all the preliminary pedagogics they could. They helped shape a soul during those years, gave it direction, and the right inoculation. All of it was intended as fortification against the day when its possessor would go off on his own; and if he hadn't already made his declaration of independence, it usually came when he went to college. The separation was tough on the boy, but tougher on parents who knew something of his deficiencies, and perhaps knew the extent of their failure with him.

The novices of the "Tommy Arkle" type understood this phenomenon as it had not been acknowledged before; they understood the turmoil that the transition brought to a freshman, as well as the resistance in the parents. Some guiding hand was needed to take the student over the hump. That was the dean's function. The independent spirit wasn't going to be checked with *thou shalts* and *thou shalt nots*. Best to give the boy some rein and let him go, with a few casual hints about the surface of the road ahead, a general itinerary, and some good man-to-man tips on the nature of the horse he was riding. He was going to make his own decisions anyway, so there was no point in imposing another's will upon him. Give him the straight dope on details he should be aware of in reaching a destination, but never tell him what the destination must be.

The philosophy paid off at Illinois, and it paid off at other colleges. Dean Clark wasn't alone. There was Briggs at Harvard preaching and practicing the same; Hawkes at Columbia; Christian Gauss at Princeton; Stanley Coulter at Purdue; Scott Goodnight at Wisconsin; John Straub at the University of Oregon, with a host of others scattered in between—deans, unrecognized and unsung at little colleges, doing just as good a job as those in the big universities. They were all guardians of undergraduates, as differentiated from the dictators and the disciplinarians. And it was not exactly a paternalistic guardianship, for they also shared the student's perspective. Young at heart, they could think and talk in terms their clientele knew. They worked *with* students, and even the best of fathers often finds that hard to do.

Having the advantage of a less personal relationship, student and dean could discuss things in a way that modesty or deference prevented father and son from talking. The confidence established between them was what counted. It was the delicacy of touch that set off the sympathetic dean from the dictatorial dean. Between the two was all the difference of surgeon and sawbones. Both types were amateurs, but the man who chose to be the guardian, the man with unending patience, a sparkle of wit, and a ready sympathy, the man who was willing to take the long chance and challenge his students to make the right choice, proved himself the stronger.

It is quite possible that the deanship during the pioneer

period would have developed into nothing more than a police agency if there hadn't been a Clark, a Hawkes, or a Briggs to point a different way. Theirs is a legacy of uncommon quality.

In accepting the guardian approach—carrying on from where parents left off—these men learned that one of the primary concerns of deans was dealing with the idiosyncrasies of fathers and mothers, as well as with the idiosyncrasies of their offspring. No two students could be treated alike, and neither could any two sets of parents. There were overindulgent parents and all-too-severe ones, the trusting kind and the suspicious, the benign and the spiteful, the domineering and the indifferent. Before a dean could do much with the problem boy, he had to make some diagnosis of the shortcomings under which he had been brought up. It was amazing to discover the number of sons who were total strangers to parents—particularly the well-heeled parents who had spent a great deal of money on summer camps and prep schools, tutoring and travel, cars and wardrobes; at the university it was merely a question of purchasing a diploma. For such spoiled brats, deans were supposed to accomplish in four years what parents had been unable to do in seventeen.

Then there was the parade of solicitous, protective mothers who couldn't bear the thought of letting their children out of sight. "Madam, we guarantee satisfaction, or we return the boy," impatiently pledged the President of Princeton, Woodrow Wilson, to a loving matron who had pestered every office on campus during the opening days of college, and still wasn't convinced that Princeton was worthy of receiving her son.[2] Deans were required to be less direct in terminating maternal soliloquies.

Fond mothers were a plague to early deans intent on establishing a tradition of self-reliance among their charges. "These eager mothers," claimed the usually un-ruffled Dean Clark, "choose their boy's clothes and com-panions, and courses of study. They map out his future and all but do his work for him. They think for him, and smooth out the way for him, and leave him no chance to develop self-direction or initiative. They get him up in the morning, and tell him when to go to bed at night. If he has a task to perform, they regularly set him to it; if he has duties and obligations, he is reminded of them before he has an opportunity to rely upon his own memory or think out his own plan of procedure. He is never allowed to for-get to be polite or prompt or thoughtful or regular when mother is by, and knowing that he will not be, he comes to depend upon the fact that if there is anything he ought to do, mother will remind him of it or call his attention to it in plenty of time, even if it is nothing more than speak-ing to a caller or changing his underwear." [3]

Fathers were less of a nuisance, but deans, eager to hurry along the weaning process, complained of them too. In middle age they were still fighting off their own youth and wanted their sons to benefit by the kind of youth they had experienced. Why should a parent who had been a great athlete suffer the embarrassment of having a boy who wanted to play the piano and read Keats in his spare time? Or why should the son of a distinguished scholar want to waste his time on baseball and Saturday-night

81

flings? What was wrong with the dean and the faculty that they couldn't mold him into a normal lad? No matter how wise the college counsel or how mutual the understanding between student and dean, from the parents' point of view, the dean was missing a golden opportunity to shape a life as it ought to be shaped.

The pioneer deans did not succeed in bringing about permanent reforms among college youth any more than they succeeded in producing a general change in American parents. It was necessary to take one student at a time, one class annually; and the next year there was a new batch on which the ritual had to be performed all over again. The critics along Main Street couldn't understand how college officials could be so inefficient that they had to contend with the same problems repeated year after year; they couldn't understand why an issue settled one autumn had to be settled all over again the following autumn. No reiterated explanations ever convinced them that annually there was a new delegation of students who had to be given a chance to learn through error and experiment the same old lessons of social adjustment.

Deans of the early 1900s set a pattern for dealing with parents and students, but they did not in any way lighten the burden that their successors would have to carry fifty years later. Superficially youth, indeed, has changed. Facilities of travel and communication, a freer social climate, the shock treatment of wars and world emergencies have brought an earlier maturity. By themselves, teenagers make choices which their parents, brought up in the protective atmosphere of family and community, have

never made even in adulthood. There are more choices and more chances for error.

Solicitous mothers, jealous of the dean's position as temporary guardian, still pour into his office. Although their concern appears to be totally outmoded, they feel that the dean should exercise more authority in insisting upon Jimmy's wearing overshoes when it snows, writing home more often, turning in at ten o'clock. Deans are called out of bed at one-thirty in the morning to explain why Alexander didn't phone home that evening; something must be drastically wrong: he always phones on Friday nights. And every year on almost every campus there are actually mothers who desert their husbands and move to off-campus apartments where they can be nearer to a precious son, where they can check on the overshoes, the underwear, and the dean. Fathers haven't changed either, but they are more likely to go to the other extreme.

"Got a bottle of whisky?" was the demand that startled a dean as he opened his front door one evening to a father he had never met before. The parents had arrived on the campus to help their son celebrate an alumni weekend, only to discover that Percival was in the hospital from a premature celebration the previous night when a home-made bomb went off in his face. They had called at the hospital, but all they had seen of the son were two discolored eyes looking through narrow slits of dressing. Mother had gone back to the hotel to collapse; father naturally headed for the dean to find out who could be blamed for the near-fatality.

He nursed along the whisky and listened to the awful truth: the bomb was a concoction of enough chemicals to demolish a small edifice, borrowed from the college laboratories and assembled in the boy's room. It was ready for conveyance to the open spaces of the campus where the detonation could be duly auditioned by a few thousand congregating alumni, but there was an accident before it left the room. The dormitory was badly shaken; the damage from fire and smoke was considerable; the only reason the amateur pyrotechnician wasn't killed or blinded was that he happened to have a chiffonier for a shield.

As the level of whisky descended in the bottle and the facts were assimilated, Percival's father finally allowed cheerfully and unsparingly: "Dean, I think it will teach him a lesson I never could." There are few fathers who take the errors of their sons so philosophically.

Dean Gauss told of the father who pleaded for special consideration in behalf of his errant son because the elder was only an "amateur parent." A dean is exposed to all classes of amateur parents: those who steal into the offices to make surreptitious inquiries about how the boy is doing and steal quietly out with the comment, "Christopher won't need to be told, of course, that we've been here"; parents who grumble about old-fashioned college regulations which prohibit underclassmen from having cars: "Paul has had his own automobile since he was a sophomore in high school, I won't deprive him of it now and you can't either; he'd be utterly lost without it"; parents who are so terribly grieved when the son gets into a drunken smash-up that they drop in at the dean's office after a visit to the hospital to leave the keys for a brand new car which will be ready for Tom as soon as he is recovered; parents who blame the college and the dean for allowing their sons to flunk a course, to go off on a bender, or attempt suicide. And there is an old confidence gag that turns up anew over and over again on the lips of fathers who have just received the expulsion notice of their sons for misdemeanors or negligence: "You can't let Adolph leave the college. It would kill his mother. Yes, it will kill her." But there is a happy ending: it turns out that she wants him back home so badly that she accepts with open arms both the spoiled boy and the disgrace he carries.

For special occasions parents recognize the dean in his role of guardian, but he goes about the business of parenting in such an unfamiliar way they are never quite sure how far he can be trusted.

4.

"TO MAKE THINGS EASY FOR THE FACULTY"

[The Dean as Educator]

AS EDUCATOR, the dean has little to do with lecture notes, term papers, and the red pencil. His operational tools (according to his clientele) are more likely to be the anxious seat, the rule book, and the heavy hand. He may swing a lot of weight and sway a great many people, but at best he is a supernumerary, so far as his part in spreading ordinary booklearning is concerned. "To make things easy for the faculty" was the excuse Harvard's Dean Briggs gave for his existence.

If justification for his place in the academic order is called for, he has the ready explanation that he is concerned with educating "the whole man"—supplementing the accomplishments of the professors. No one has ever performed a successful autopsy to determine which parts of the whole student are infected by the faculty and which by the dean's office, but presumably the two influences, working together under ideal conditions, create the exemplary candidate for a baccalaureate degree.

Every college official, from the chancellor to the night

watchman, entertains his own notions of just what undergraduate education should include and some of the idealism stretches almost to nobility, but the dean's distinctions outdo them all in elasticity. He agrees with the professors who insist that the pith of education has to come from the classroom, agrees with the committee on student life that the extracurriculum is important too, agrees with the coaches and the alumni that physical prowess should not be neglected, and with the janitors who think that somehow the college should make gentlemen out of the dormitory inmates. The dean accepts these concepts and more, tries to shuffle them into place, compress them into something more substantial than theory, and apply them to the individual. His first responsibility is always for the individual, the whole individual, for only by sending to the classroom well-integrated individuals is he going to make it easier for the faculty. If it weren't for his terror of raising another howl of dissention from the professors, he would be more glib in revealing the secret that a very large part of a student's education has nothing to do with scholarship.

He is concerned with the intangibles that go into the making of student character, personality, and spiritual equanimity, as well as the tangibles that promote physical, social, and economic well-being. He has to consider the development of qualities such as integrity, loyalty, industry, courage, and common civility. All these are incorporated in the dean's educational design. He is responsible for both individual and group morale, for communicating to a thousand or to ten thousand students the essence of what a particular college, as a family, stands for. And he can't worry about the multitude he never sees: he has learned from experience that students are the most communicative clan in the world, and that the truth he impresses upon one is mysteriously conveyed to fifty or five hundred.

Since their superiors provided only the vaguest directives on the part this peripheral educator was to carry, deans themselves have been trying for fifty years to puzzle out what is expected of them, and no two have ever arrived at exactly the same conclusion. "We merely carry out the wishes of the administration," argues one. "Fie! our first loyalty must be to the faculty," contends another. "Nonsense, we're primarily defenders of the best interests of the students," echoes a dissenting chorus. Reaching for a compatible middle ground, Dean Donald DuShane of the University of Oregon comes up with a pat definition to which no one can object: "A student-minded or student-oriented faculty member who has administrative responsibilities." And, he adds, "That puts us squarely in the middle of students, teaching faculty members, and administrative faculty members. Our role in the center is to serve as interpreters or catalysts in relation to the fundamental functions of a college or university; a center position where we must be, in effect, custodians of the best interests of all; maybe, in a way, the cohesive element in the institution." [1]

The one point of concurrence is "education"; all deans agree at least that they are educators, and they generally accept the sententious set of principles approved by their national association, that "education encompasses the student's whole development towards a full and balanced

89

maturity, that each student's education is primarily his own responsibility, and that personnel services must function as an integral part of the total college program." According to this declaration, the dean "plans and works with faculty, staff and students for recognition of these principles. . . . He contributes to students' understanding and acceptance of the standards, requirements, and customs of the educational institution, promotes the development of a campus community which provides broad social opportunities for all . . . seeks also to provide opportunity for students to gain experience in democratic living, in self-determination, in cooperative endeavor and in leadership . . . helps to establish effective communication of student needs, interests and opinions to the faculty and administration, and insists upon fairness, honesty, and due respect for the dignity and welfare of students."[2]

There is no agreement either on or off campus that the "dignity" of students needs a professional defender, but the principles, taken as a whole, find supporters even among the topside administrators—although there is little real satisfaction among the left-handed educators in the dean's office with their application of the principles. Perennially they are so preoccupied with new emergencies and new frustrations for which there are no ground rules that the lofty ideals are sometimes overlooked. However, there have been intermissions when deans actually felt that they were serving more as educators than as umpires in a big juvenile free-for-all.

Depending on the seriousness of purpose that students supply, education has its good years and its lean, its productive periods and its less fruitful. Alert college officials watch as nervously for general upswings in undergraduate attitudes as Wall Street watches for a bull market, for these unpredictable turns in student temperament can make all the difference between quality and mediocrity in scholarship; they can last for an academic month or an academic decade, and can very clearly dictate the nature of the trials and tribulations that will harry them.

Vintage years for deans as educators were those of the depression decade of the 1930s. After the 1929 crash the campus playboys turned in their roadsters, the Charleston lost its lilt, the fraternity bootlegger was fired, and the seniors sauntered back to the library. The era of flaming youth was spent. So grim was the employment prospect for future college graduates that even the Carnegie Foundation suggested "Before making lawyers, doctors, and engineers of our boys, our educational institutions should try to find out whether there is a reasonable chance of their finding an opportunity to work." With more realism than cynicism, editorial writers kept reminding colleges that they "might as well go back to Latin, Greek and Medieval Logic and limit themselves to a few students."

The cut-back in enrollment was indeed critical. Student rosters fell off so alarmingly that the very survival of smaller liberal arts institutions appeared to be at stake. Yet the seriousness of purpose among the men who remained was so profound that deans at last were given an opportunity to serve in their preferred capacity as educators. "For a while," sighed Dean Lancaster of the University of Alabama, "it may become our privilege to devote our talents, such as they are, to advising and counseling

with our students and to postpone some of our disciplinary duties until the depression is over."

Deans everywhere had that privilege. College education became a luxury for the sons of the rich—no longer
wealthy; for sons who had always been obliged to work
their way, it became something of a battle. Tuition in the
better private colleges was advanced to $250 and $300 a
year, and a dormitory room could cost as much a $40 or
$50 a semester. That was too much. Careful students
rented off-campus apartments, cooked their own meals,
and made their own beds at costs running as high as
$3.50 a week per man. Threadbare jackets were almost as
common as coonskin coats had been during the 1920s. To
keep fraternity houses open, pledge chairmen were begging freshmen to join, instead of offering snobbish invitations.

At Beloit Dean Alderman saw the last of the big expensive fraternity and class splurges and remarked: "To have
discovered that programs can be homemade, that orches-
tras can be smaller, that victrola and radio parties are a
possibility is almost a spiritual achievement. I have seen
vague evidence once or twice which suggested that jazz
mania was giving way to jig-saw-mania. When an old-
fashioned taffy-pull begins to show itself now and then on
a sophisticated campus, one has a feeling that unless
things get better soon, some group some place will revert
to the innocent diversion of charades."

Typical of hundreds of penniless students in other colleges was a Beloit freshman wearing sweat shirts and
trousers discarded by his high school athletic department,
shifting from room to room, from table to table in search

of board and room that was a few cents cheaper, and looking for any kind of menial job that would pay for both. "Through the effort of the employment bureau," Dean Alderman reported, "he was given work in a down-town restaurant for his meals and in a home for his room. When, a few weeks later, his landlady could not pay her utility bills, her water and electricity were shut off; and when she could no longer buy coal for heat, the boy had to leave. As if this were not enough, the proprietor at the restaurant found an applicant among the young unemployed who, in desperation, was willing to work nine hours a day, seven days a week, for his board and two dollars. The student, through no neglect or incompetency, was again a dependent. Within a few days after he was settled in a new home where he had a furnace job, his new landlady had a chance to rent the same room to two younger men who would care for the furnace and pay her a small sum in addition. The student was again homeless." [3]

Boys had a way of maturing rapidly under sobering conditions of this sort. Such industrious, conscientious, sober-minded students hadn't crossed college campuses for decades, and deans for once had the gratification of giving assistance that contributed toward direct acquirement of an education. To their offices the depression years brought an endless line of hard-luck cases, complaints about the quality of instruction, and the atmosphere of a social welfare office. There was a run on scholarships and loan funds. The Federal Emergency Relief Administration providentially came to the rescue with work projects that paid munificent wages of $15 a month

—a godsend that kept the indigent busy with every type of chore from chopping trees to painting murals, and also kept them in college. Deans were overwhelmed with the trivia of government red tape, petty accounts, and petty background investigations, but no one complained for the effort brought visible rewards.

It was a wonderful relief from service as liquor control agent, censor for bawdy contributions to the comic magazine, and nursemaid to the playboys. "These students who have come out of the depression are a great crowd," declared Dean Fred Turner of Illinois in 1935. "They are an interested crowd. They are a decent group. And they are less selfish than you would think. I investigated sixty of their cases last year for qualifications for F.E.R.A. work, and each one said that, though he needed the work badly, if someone needed it more than he did, he would try to get along. The students of the depression seem to me to come nearer to my idea of what real university students should be than any group that I have observed in the seventeen years I have been observing them." [4]

Far more astonishing than the depression lads, however, was the legion of war veterans who took possession of the campuses fifteen years later. Instead of an eager few there was an eager many. No dean anticipated their arrival with any enthusiasm, for men who had lived with the violence of war would bring the products of that life back with them. After the Revolution it had taken Yale, Harvard, and Princeton the best part of a decade to get back to normal. The moral disruption of the Civil War was worse. In 1945 older deans remembered that the Student Army Training Corps program of 1918 had produced "the dumbest lot of students ever congregated around centers of learning" and that the doughboys of World War I had been anything but a salutary influence. They dreaded the day when a new generation of ex-soldiers would return from Europe and the Pacific, not to mention those who had suffered only the boredom of camps and bases scattered over continental U.S.A. Survivors of wars inevitably upset the professor's applecart and the dean's. A mob of arrogant conquering heroes blessed with fat government subsidies could be counted on to damage the cause of higher education beyond repair.

Dean Scott Goodnight of Wisconsin, who had been on the job a long time, tried to conceal some of his pessimism for the future, but in 1944 he warned his colleagues: "In 1919, the demoralization produced by the S.A.T.C., the sharp recoil upon escape from the repression of military discipline on the part of returned soldiers and sailors, and the new and unwelcome restraints imposed by Prohibition, all conspired to bring upon us in the colleges a period of very bad morale, of resistance to any and every type of discipline, of complete rejection of the principle of self-discipline, of reckless pleasure-seeking and extravagance—of more or less open contempt for scholastic attainments. . . . These evils burst upon us with a violence that had never been even approximately felt before the war. . . . The opening of the college year in 1919 was simply a bedlam of excitement—of fraternity rushing, of hazing and whooping it up.

"There are millions more men in service now than there were then. They will have been in service longer. They will have been in service in every clime, in every part of

the globe. More of them will have cracked, nervously and
mentally, under that prolonged strain, that terrific ordeal.
From these distant climes, where they will have been located for two, three, or four years, they are going to bring
home mores, concepts, behavior patterns that will amaze
us. . . . Those with combat experience will offer the
greater problems. They have been living in an atmosphere
of great tension. It is going to be a hard and slow process
to return to the relaxations of normal life. . . . We must
expect after this war is over a repetition of the troubles
which followed World War I. The only difference is that
the mess will be far worse than it was the other time. . . .
Those responsible for meeting and advising and counseling these young old men will have their hands full. . . .
It is going to be a time to try men's souls." [5]

During the last year or two of the war, the wounded
and the unfit began trickling back, while the deans were
still trying to line up the committees, counselors, and psychiatrists that were going to handle them. Because the
numbers were small, the problems were not insurmountable, but there were enough to give a foretaste of what
was to come. The quiet of a New England college town
was shattered with the news that a South Pacific hero
wearing three battle stars and a dozen ribbons objected
to taking suggestions from the local police, and in response to friendly overtures about alcoholic behavior, the
sophomore ex-Marine had not only defied and slugged
the honored chief of police, but felled him and left him
sprawled across Main Street. At Michigan State a dean
proudly launching his ideal rehabilitation program for
veterans was rebuked by one of his patients with the snarl:

"Why the hell do you keep telling us to go see a psychiatrist?" And at a college to the west, a trio of former bluejackets, reverting to familiar freedoms of wartime, picked up the address of a brothel from a genial bar philosopher, had a few more drinks and headed down a side street. But at the address they had been given a masculine young English instructor opened the door, rather than a madam; jumping to the conclusion that it was improper for faculty members to frequent such places, the trio proceeded to throw him out on his ear and claim the bathrobed blonde in the background. Too late they discovered that the address supplied by the cooperative barfly represented a faculty apartment house, and the blonde was a chaste faculty wife.

Deans assumed that they were in for half a decade of this sort of thing.

More of the expected occurred in September 1945. Paul Simons had been a second-string linesman and upcoming politician of his junior class back in 1941. During the four intervening years he had seen a large segment of the globe with the Army Air Force. He had flown the Hump and accidentally won an assortment of honors, decorations, and a second lieutenant's commission. A week ahead of most of his fellow veterans, he foresightedly arrived back on his campus, sniffed at the dormitory-full of 4Fs who were finishing up the summer quarter, and decided the college needed the kind of leadership it had forfeited in 1941. Lieutenant Simons was the man.

He rallied a handful of non-coms and gobs who were feeling their way into the awkward readjustment period with the patronizing proposal: "Let's take over the place."

Over the beers, a new order for the old college was blue-printed. They were to be the nucleus for an omnipotent student government organized to settle the differences with the administration that were bound to develop. They could easily overlook the 4Fs, initiate other GIs as they arrived. There was no question about it, if they stuck together they could run things their own way, get anything they wanted, without kowtowing to the dean or being bothered by his antiquated regulations. They had been through hell for four years; the faculty owed them a break now.

Paul Simons' regime lasted less than a week. He had grossly underestimated the caliber of his student associates—underestimated them almost as badly as had the dean and all the committees. Student politicking was kid stuff; they wanted no part of it. Nor were they interested in all the other hokum on which they had wasted their time before the war. The few Paul Simonses on American campuses were pathetically outnumbered.

Contrary to the almost hysterical premonitions, the "young old men" in the faded khaki shirts turned out to be the finest and the most cooperative assortment of students deans had ever known. And they arrived with a purpose. They had a lot of time to make up, and wanted to spend it with the books. From the galaxy of former football stars, the coaches had a hard time assembling enough material for a first-rate team. Projectors of other activities experienced similar troubles, but wherever the veterans found an outmoded or inefficient student government, they became the promoters of new constitutions, accepting legislative and judicial responsibilities that had never

99

before been yielded to undergraduates. During the war, fraternities had almost reached the point of extinction and the attitude among many veterans was to let them die, but when they saw that the houses were needed for living quarters, they pitched in like old executives to restore the chapters on a firmer, more democratic basis.

When consulted by faculty advisers, individual GIs knew exactly the subject in which they wanted to concentrate, and they didn't care to have the program diluted with snap courses. During the long years overseas they had decided on a profession and were eager to get started on the way toward it. Far more complaints came to the dean about inadequacies of instruction than about abusive demands from professors. In coeducational institutions where co-eds had once tallied consistently superior grades, the men began to edge them.

It wasn't a question of getting a degree for the sake of a B.S. or a B.A.; they wanted to acquire what went with it. One freshman had already been graduated from another college; he insisted on being permitted to start in all over again to earn a degree that meant something. An older married student, who had never spent a day in high school, had been catching up while in the army. He passed the Armed Forces Institute tests with flying colors and entered college. The world needed ministers and he was intent on being one, so he selected a philosophy major, accepted a rural pastorate, moved into the empty parsonage, and preached a weekly sermon for four years while carrying his courses on the side. He was graduated close to the top of his class. A thirty-four-year-old man, who had dropped out of college fifteen years before for lack of funds, came back to start the long grind for a career in medicine. A brigadier general, originally in the class of 1921, returned as a junior in the same class with his son.

Altogether the veterans of World War II gave the deans the greatest challenge they had ever known. To be sure, it was necessary to contend with flings, beer busts, and outbreaks, but combustion no longer occupied the center of the stage and when the affairs were over the participants were ready to go back to work and let the dean regain his peace of mind. Problems of housing shortages, classroom shortages, and staff shortages were incessant. A college could estimate that it might have nine thousand possible applications for nine hundred places. One in every ten of the veterans came back with a wife and they were looking for an apartment or a place to park their trailers, so the deans went into the real-estate business. The Veterans Administration was helping in a big way and called for a campus liaison officer—the dean. Charity organizations and the churches wanted to help and needed someone through whom they could work— the dean. Faculty committees laboring on instruction programs had to have the key man on student problems in their membership—the dean.

"Most of us have discovered that some of our teaching methods, our paternalistic attitudes, our disciplinary systems, and our social organizations are out of focus with the veteran," Dean Neidlinger of Dartmouth summarized, in 1946. "Their purpose and motivation is unusual; they have very strong vocational interests; the marriage problems are new and big. . . . In the past we labored under

101

a great handicap caused by the indifference of many students to the opportunities offered to them and by the extent of their disinterest in intellectual acitvity. . . . The veterans know what they want, and they are determined to get it. The quantity and quality of the academic work they turn out is prodigious. It is an inspiration to have them in class. . . . In the past it was a little disreputable to ask questions or to consult instructors outside of class. Now they pump the professor and contribute pertinent observations from their own experience. . . . They have seen what many instructors have only read about. These mature students have acquired a sense of values; they are not fooled by the false front hiding a weak man, a weak argument or a fatuous idea. They have learned much of themselves, and they can recognize a fathead, a stuffed shirt, a charlatan, or a pretender a mile off. They have learned that when the chips are down what a man *is* is more important than what he does for a living or where his father was born. . . . A lot of academic Sacred Cows have been slaughtered to feed the Army and the Navy."[6]

No one has ever given a very satisfactory answer as to what produced this phenomenon—why the veterans of World War II were a breed entirely different from veterans of other wars. Maturity was hastened by the impressive weight of responsibility they had carried and by the sobering effect of the tragedies witnessed, but the men of 1918 and 1865 had corresponding experience for the time. The indulgences of GIs between 1941 and 1945 were the same indulgences armies have always known, and were abandoned with similar reluctance. Leverage of the GI bill was considerable, but the colleges would have been almost as crowded without it. The competition for a classroom chair and for a dormitory room furnished an incentive, but not an explanation. On the basis of experience of the past, colleges had every reason to anticipate the kind of disruption that Dean Goodnight outlined. If the multitude of veterans had shown more of the churlish arrogance of the 1918 doughboys, they would have made a shambles of American colleges. Instead they advanced the cause of education by a decade.

The postwar years, like the depression period, demonstrated what a dean could accomplish with a body of serious students possessing educational purpose. Relieved of some of the harassments of the hellraisers, their parents, and the troublemakers, he was able to work constructively with individuals who needed and who could profit by his assistance. He was still only a left-handed peripheral educator, but he was making things a little easier for the faculty, and furnishing the assistance that enabled students to draw out the best in themselves. Over and over again in the middle '30s and late '40s young alumni dropped into the dean's office to remind him of some forgotten word of counsel or some forgotten material assistance: "You may not know it, Dean, but I never would have made it, if it hadn't been for you."

5.

"I HOPE THE MAN WILL SEEK THE OFFICE AND NOT THE OFFICE THE MAN"

[*The Dean as Counselor*]

IN ITS DISPLAY of human frailties and virtues, an undergraduate body in college is a fair cross section of a youthful population anywhere else. Perhaps it ought not to be so—perhaps collegians should be the cream of the crop, with the dolts, the disillusioned, and the indisposed eliminated, but it never works out that way. Despite the meticulous sifting of admissions officers, applicants with personality and character defects do "get in," and somehow they can make themselves more conspicuous than the wholesome majority and the self-propelled eggheads.

There are the unscrupulous to match the honorable, the extroverts and the introverts, the laggards and the conscientious, the naïve and the sophisticated, the conformists and nonconformists—with a seasoning of psychos, perverts, and rabblerousers. Fond parents, eager to send an unscathed son to a campus isolated from the ills and iniquities of mankind, will not find their utopia on this planet. Universities of the best academic standing were ever thus.

It is the task of deans and faculty advisers to reconcile the individuals in this heterogeneous company to some kind of manageable conformity—a conformity consistent with traditional educational standards and the standards which students in their better moments know they would like to possess. The reconciliation process is known to the trade as "counseling": among old-timers and unaffected laymen it is spoken of quite simply as "helping young folks get on." By some it is regarded as a science, by others as an art, but whether artist or scientist is performing, humility of approach is all-essential. In the most gratifying reformation of a student, there is no room for smugness. The counselor showing telltale signs of a craving for credit or prestige can be summarily dismissed as a humbug and a pharisee.

"Lifting men into themselves is your chief work," expounded Purdue's dean emeritus Stanley Coulter to a gathering of younger deans some twenty-five years ago. "Unless you have that conception, you haven't the conception that makes a dean of men. There is not one bit of effective work that you have done under any rules. You have done the effective work because you are a man, and because you had deep in your heart, higher than any social preferment, higher than any social advances or academic advances, the welfare of those men with whom you come in contact. You haven't set up discipline as the chief objective of your work. Discipline is the last resort. Yours is an occupation that has in it more possibilities for touching human life, for uplifting human life, for making

105

the world what it ought to be, than any other occupation that is given to man to enter upon. Your primary function is to introduce youth to its own best self." [1]

Those were the ideals for counseling set by the early exemplars and they have not changed materially—except that mechanics for surer diagnosis of ailments have been perfected, and a less personal approach is preferred by the new school of professionals. A battalion of specialized counselors, psychologists, and examiners in many an institution has been organized into a complex personnel service, intuitional philosophies have given way to modern doctrines of the behavioral sciences, but in most colleges there is still a dean of men or his equivalent ready to give the old-fashioned kind of personal counsel Coulter advocated.

Almost prayerfully Dean Briggs implored as he was taking over at Harvard: "I hope the man will seek the office and not the office the man."[2] His hope was so fully realized that he was all but overwhelmed and exhausted. The voluntary search for counsel is the important thing, and students don't go to the dean of their own accord in response to advertisements that his door is always open, or in response to public pronouncements regarding the invaluable assistance he can give. Through the slow process of cultivating confidence and acquiring a reputation for knowing some of the answers he has to earn his following, and once he has proved his worth as a counselor, he will know no peace.

One such distraught dean totted up the problems brought to him in a three-hour afternoon and compared notes with a local doctor who in the same period had treated everything from mumps and pneumonia to canker and endocarditis. They decided they had something in common. On the dean's listing were: an injudicious freshman set on marrying a waitress of doubtful character at an off-campus hash house; a brilliant junior determined to quit college to join the Marines; a pre-med major who had decided to abandon a career in dentistry for nightclub crooning; the chronic griper sounding off on the injustice of his biology professor's marking system; the experimenter in search of advice on treatment for a venereal disease; the sharper demanding a campus license for selling razor blades; a casualty on crutches wanting to go over the legal complications of an automobile crackup; a stricken sophomore looking for sympathy on the impending divorce of his parents; the eager beaver seeking wisdom on the comparative merits of summer employment as a garage mechanic and attendance at an art school; the penitent ready to confess that it was he who stole the Tally-Ho Tavern sign; a wild-eyed bookworm on the verge of a nervous breakdown because he had overslept a Latin quiz—the first class he had ever cut.

For such everyday enigmas dropped on the dean's desk, the professional literature on counseling furnishes no ready-made, pat solutions. Every problem calls for a very special kind of profound understanding in the light of college record, psychological test scores, family background, ambitions for the future; and there is no minimizing the significance of one case compared to another. When all the ramifications are aired, it may turn out that the penitent who overslept the Latin test is a neurotic with the most deep-seated emotional complications of all, and the would-be salesman of safety razors is in much greater need of moral rearmament than of spare cash, for his sole purpose in selling razors is to pay off his gambling debts.

"I wish I could forget the thousands of occasions in which I was alone with my God," reflected Dean Ray Warnock of Penn State, after years of listening to student confidences and contending with student predicaments. "I would have liked to share the responsibility with the President of the College, with the psychologist, the physician, but I had to say, 'No, you are it. You have to make that decision.' I have no doubt that there are thousands of Penn State graduates who are where they are now—for better or worse—because of some decision I helped them to make when I was, like a country doctor, alone with my God." [3]

The doctor has one advantage over the dean. He makes his diagnosis, offers a prescription, and imposes his dietary restrictions; but a competent dean exercises no such authority. The ultimate remedy for a student's malady—if the cure is to take hold—has to be drawn from the patient himself. The dean as counselor asks a great many questions, some of them leading; he applies a little first aid, explores all the symptoms, inquires into circumstances, pokes and prods, suggests the kind of relief that might help, but in the end both the diagnosis and the curative program come from the client. Of course, it would be far easier to dictate the obvious remedy—momentarily much easier for the student, too—but that would be like furnishing the answer for the math problem, cheating a student out of an educational opportunity, not "introducing youth to its own best self." However, there is no single routine for counseling; every case demands a special procedure; and, as in medicine, the accepted diagnostic methods and the approved palliatives of one year are out of fashion the next.

To illuminate the importance of getting a student to unravel his own problem, Dean Clark of Illinois liked to use the illustration of the obstinate Bill Henderson, a desperately poor senior who called at his office a few months before graduation to explain that he couldn't go through with it. One reverse had followed another; college woes were multiplied by difficulties at home. His last dollar was gone and there was no point in trying to graduate. The struggle was utterly futile.

Patiently the dean went over the implications, pointing out how much would be lost by forfeiting a year's work almost completed. He offered to help with a loan and to lighten some of his work load, but Bill wasn't to be swayed. Clark finally acknowledged defeat himself and conceded that the man was a free agent; nobody could prevent his leaving. They shook hands on the decision and Henderson withdrew.

Late in the afternoon the dean too left his office for the night, and as he locked the door, noticed his customer of the afternoon standing at the end of the corridor looking out the window, a stiff back toward him. He had to pass within three feet of Henderson, and the temptation to make some friendly allusion to their long session was almost irresistible, but the dean coldly walked by without so much as a "Good night."

The next morning Henderson was back in the office. He was ready to take up the dean on his offer to help with a

109

loan. Shyly he added: "If you had spoken to me last night, it would really have been the end. I had to fight it out again by myself, and a single word would have been enough to make me quit. I realize now it would have been a foolish decision."

Every dean has experienced similar situations and occasionally the student does leave college. More frequently, if the dean hasn't used his influence too persuasively, the truant gets halfway home, to the next town, to the edge of campus before he turns back.

By spring of his sophomore year at a small eastern college "Hasty" Erickson had against him an accumulation of counts that were bothersome even to his own retractable conscience. He was failing half of his courses, drinking too much, running around with the wrong crowd, and, unlike most such students, fully conversant with all his shortcomings. In his frequent sessions with the dean, he was uncommonly frank and honest, always confiding more details of his exploits than was necessary, and expressing his intentions of settling down. But Hasty never settled down. Through accident or indiscretion, he was involved in a next scrape before penance for the last could be served, and invariably he was the ringleader, a natural executive capable of swinging a great deal of constructive influence on the campus, but rarely demonstrating that kind of capability. To his credit, he could be counted on to take the side of the underdog—but the wrong dog—defending an indefensible cause, and that meant getting needlessly involved in more trouble. In practically every call at the dean's office he forthrightly volunteered to withdraw from college as a penalty for his latest misdemeanor, but that was the easy way out for Hasty, quite unacceptable to the dean.

Finally, just before June examinations Hasty got into some real trouble with the law. One of his best friends was taken into custody by the sheriff and jailed for the night on charges that were incontestable. Hasty had a great urge to chat with his unfortunate buddy and offer him the comfort a good friend deserved. Two late-evening appeals to the sheriff for permission to visit the cell were denied; it was past visiting hours. So Hasty, with two confederates, turned to the bottle for vicarious solace and by two o'clock the trio had convinced themselves that no sheriff had the right to separate such staunch partners. Together they returned to the lockup, aroused a very irate jailor, and demanded entrance. In the scuffle that ensued, the jailor succeeded in defending his bastille, but only at the expense of a badly battered door. The mission of the stormers was not accomplished, and they were wise enough to escape the scene before a riot squad descended.

To all his other imputations Hasty Erickson had now added one that was unique—breaking into jail. Once more he decided the time had come to leave college, and the dean didn't disagree, but the offender was at last under serious indictment, released on bail, with a court trial coming up in a few days. Since he was an out-of-state student, the authorities wanted to make very sure that he wasn't going to skip town. The dean took the risk of vouching for him, placed him on disciplinary probation —in addition to the scholastic probation already on the record—and then offered a reckless bet that he couldn't pass his finals.

111

Hasty had already made up his mind that he was through with the tribulations of college, and no penalty more distasteful than going through with the examinations could have been proposed. Yet he didn't have it in him to pass up a sporting wager. It was pretty late in the year to make amends, but immediately he pulled himself together, started to cram, memorize, and indulge in all-night grinds as he had never been known to indulge before. On his own, he paid the sheriff a tactful visit and made such a disarming apology that even the hard-hearted upholder of the law was touched. He miraculously passed his examinations, got off the hook with a reasonable court fine, paid for repairs on the jail door, and went home.

The dean had counseled and counseled Hasty with no visible results, but he wasn't ready to give up. He was still convinced the student could be converted into a first-rate campus citizen and refused to dismiss him despite the fact that if he returned to college the following year he would be on both disciplinary and scholastic probation. So the counselor took another long, long chance, and when Hasty finally received a summer letter from the dean's office it was not a dismissal notice, rather it was an invitation to serve as proctor in a freshman dormitory, an honor accorded only to the most promising student leaders. Hasty read the letter at home, went to his room, and cried.

He arrived back on campus early the following September and had such a warm welcome for his dormitory charges, was so helpful in rustling luggage and offering sound counsel to freshmen that even parents called at the dean's office to commend the college on its choice of big-hearted proctors. Hasty was a new man, and a champion of faculty rules and regulations.

On most of the counseling problems with which deans have been faced recurrently over a period of fifty years they have remained remarkably loyal to fundamental policies set by their predecessors in office. But they have budged on a few issues. Marriage and studenthood, for instance, were irreconcilable until the late 1940s; colleges generally were located in isolated residential communities and students were expected to reside in dormitories or fraternity houses where they could live the prescribed life of celibacy. "Marriage for undergraduates remains, as I see it, a desperate remedy to be resorted to only in otherwise hopeless cases," asserted Princeton's Dean Gauss in 1930, without being too specific on what he meant by "hopeless cases."[4]

The veterans of World War II changed all that. College executives discovered that students living in the glow of matrimony often were much more likely candidates for Phi Beta Kappa keys than those exposed to the freedoms of a dormitory, and that young grooms who had been serious disciplinary problems as bachelors became paragons of academic propriety under the influence of a bride. Instead of being regarded as outcasts of the college community, married students began to be a welcome component, and universities were soon erecting apartment houses for their accommodation.

Deans still have a lot of pryingly personal questions to ask when a student with matrimony in mind calls on him for counsel, and the answer isn't the unqualified *no* it

113

used to be. But deans are on the losing end of this new sociological trend. Their appointment calendars are complicated with a great many invitations to weddings, christenings, and trial-and-error apartment dinners given by the newlyweds to provide evidence that the marriage was at least gastronomically advantageous. The steady income in complimentary cigars does not quite compensate for the outlay in silver spoons for babies, and the reduction in bachelor quandaries hardly makes up for the assessment in connubial conundrums to be solved. Almost a quarter of American undergraduates now get a marriage license before they get a diploma. At New Mexico A and M, where over a third of the student body is married, Dean Philip Ambrose echoes an increasingly familiar complaint that his problems "run the gamut from husband and wife fights to supposed peeping Toms, to husbands playing around with other husbands' wives, and wives playing around with other wives' husbands." Marriage hasn't yet become a panacea for college dilemmas.

For years the stock answer to appeals for permission to drive a jalopy to college was a negative as emphatic as the one for marriage, but as the car and the broad highway took possession of the country, the deans finally broke down, permitted student cars conditionally, and then began removing the conditions. Princeton and Oberlin are among the few private institutions that are still resolutely attempting to keep undergraduates out of the driver's seat.

In 1926 the General Faculty at Oberlin brooded long and thoughtfully over the menace of the motor vehicle and came up with the typical conclusion: "Waste of time, absence from classes, and neglect of college work are much more prevalent among students who have the use of motor-cars while in college than in the student body as a whole; failures in studies are more numerous among such students, and as a body their scholastic standing averages lower than that of other students; there have recently been several serious cases of college discipline directly traceable to the use of cars; the growing congestion of cars about the campus is becoming a menace, and injury to the campus and other property from cars driven and parked upon it is a source of dissatisfaction and expense to the college; the danger of fatal accidents on the highways from the use of antiquated and untrustworthy cars as some students are using is very great."

Oberlin forbade student cars and became a collegiate bicycle and motor-scooter center of the United States. Almost annually appeals to lift the restrictions are made by the cyclists, and Dean Holdeman is kept at wits' end trying to hold the line. So far he has been successful, although agitation for Thunderbirds, MGs, and Volkswagens is winning elsewhere.

Universities with tremendous numbers of commuting students, dependent on private transportation, set the pace, and the rules are now being made by the traffic engineers, the parking-lot attendants, and the campus cops rather than the deans.

Ideas have changed too on student drinking. After Prohibition was repealed in 1933 a wait-and-see-what-happens attitude was prevalent in administrative circles. "Every time you make a rule, you relieve a student of just so much moral obligation," was the common view. "The emphasis should be placed on what the student ought to do in order to develop into a decent citizen and a self-respecting individual, and he has got to do that himself. The institution can't do it. Let him arrive at a conclusion in any way that he sees fit, but hold him to an early arrival." [5] There was an element of expediency as well as idealism in that stand—expediency, irresolution, and postponement. Unquestionably liquor would have been summarily banned if there had been any sure way of enforcing a campus prohibition, but there wasn't.

It took two decades for deans to get off the fence. Most of them are off now, scattered on both sides of the fence. A single can of beer found in a fraternity house at Stanford, for example, is sufficient evidence to close the doors of that fraternity permanently, while across the nation at a more liberal college, a dean is regarded as a pretty gloomy fellow if he can't make the rounds of house cocktail parties along with faculty members and students. No resolution of this inconsistency is yet in sight, although it is recognized that about 75 per cent of all disciplinary cases involve drinking.

Taken together, automobiles and alcohol account for the dean's most tormenting headaches, for on a lively week end the automobile extends the range of student activity over a longitudinal five hundred miles, and alcohol extends the range of student fantasy an equal latitudinal distance. Monday in the dean's office is the bruising day of the week when the refinements of patient counseling are most likely to be overlooked.

Strictly amateur were the old deans, trying to cope with the confusion of predicaments into which students

wedged themselves. At first they were recruited most frequently from the English department, but presidents soon discovered that an equally reliable dean could be borrowed from the chemistry lab, from the German classroom, from mathematics, history, or philosophy. No field of learning was entirely safe from expropriation. "Someone waved a wand one morning," quipped Paul Eaton of California Tech, "and by evening I was a dean." [6]

Periodically there are runs on the athletic department, and an ex-athlete who is thoroughly enjoying life as a coach of swimming, track, or football one year will be enjoying it less the next as a counselor and disciplinarian. They are drawn from the nonacademic world too: from politics and business, from journalism and engineering. Roman Catholic priests, retired naval officers, welfare workers with juvenile delinquents, Marine Corps chaplains answer the call. One excellent personnel man found that a dozen years as a creator of animated cartoons provided just the right background for deaning, and another gave up the confining administration of a poultry farm only to find that administering student personnel was much more confining.

Almost any previous experience can be turned to good account in the vineyard of counseling. A foreign student from Nigeria, for example, was giving Dean Milton L. Hinga a hard time at Hope College in Holland, Michigan. After a summer's indoctrination in Chicago, the African lad entered so wholeheartedly and so conspicuously into a program of righting all the wrongs to which his race was subjected in America that he was doing far more harm than good to the cause. Dean Hinga had spent twenty-five years as a track coach before taking up his new profession and saw in his problem student the makings of a crack runner. Tactfully he began redirecting the zealot's eagerness from the platform to the cinders. Under Hinga's tutelage, the Nigerian gradually scrapped his personal crusade to realign the human races and became the champion two-miler in the Michigan Intercollegiate Athletic Association—and something of a sensation too, for he would have nothing to do with spikes: he insisted on running barefoot.

Among the old-timers there was a common conviction about working with students: the motivation of the individual was all-important. College life was a prolongation of adolescence, a postponement of adulthood, and the idea was to inspire the boy to shorten that postponement by choosing a definite purpose to which his college endeavors could be attached. A student was in turmoil until he found himself, until he acquired a sense of identity and a sense of basic values, until he decided upon a life aim. College was a place where he could most readily establish those values and find that aim.

What a student got out of college depended on his motivation, and that motivation usually had a vocational basis. A boy needed to pin his endeavor on some tangible purpose. That did not mean discrediting the value of a liberal education; rather the chemistry major had to be shown how courses in fine arts or economics would have bearing on his future professional status—his cultural standard of living—and the fine arts or economics majors had to be shown how they would benefit correspondingly from work in chemistry.

"It is true," Dean Hawkes pointed out, "that if you took the law away from many lawyers—just peeled it off—or the medicine from some physicians, or the engineering from certain engineers, or the scholarship from certain college professors, you would have a pretty naked person left." [7] He wanted to prevent that kind of nakedness.

"There is no way of deciding what to do with a boy apart from his preferences, his abilities, his likes and his dislikes," Dean Clark emphasized. "The greatest handicap of all is the handicap of mental and physical indifference—in plain language, laziness. Very few people are lazy when they are doing something that interests them immensely. A man will not be addicted to laziness and indifference in college if he can make up his mind fairly early what he wants most to do in life." [8]

All of these educational counselors regarded their work in helping students find themselves as a sort of ministry, quite unrelated to any science. It never occurred to them that a man could be torn apart psychologically to get at his difficulties. Given a sound objective and a fresh spirit, a student of character would overcome his problems. The objective and the high character were all-important. A dean seldom used crutches like psychological examinations, interest tests, and personality inventories in his counseling. The appropriate tools were common sense, tact, and intuition; they were marvelously effective, but, lacking professional understanding of human behavior, the analysts sometimes made some amazing blunders.

Just as the amateur deans were breaking into the field of counseling, the scientists were invading it from another direction. In 1899 the president of the University of

Chicago, William Rainey Harper, had brought a laugh to the old guard of the academic world by announcing that one of the most urgent needs in education was "the scientific study of the student himself," his character, his characteristics, his educational capacity, his tastes, his social nature. "Provision must be made," Harper insisted, "either by the regular instructors or by those appointed especially for the purpose, to study in detail the man or woman to whom education is offered." He went so far as to predict that within fifty years, the neglected scientific study of students would become a major academic endeavor.[9]

To professors schooled in the impersonal German tradition a pronouncement of this sort was the height of administrative revery, insulting to the dignity of the teaching profession. Nobody took Dr. Harper very seriously— except the psychologists, and they were already deeply engaged in that scientific study. Within a few years they informed their incredulous colleagues that intelligence and aptitudes could be measured, that science could help predict success or failure for a student; testing procedures were inseparable from effective counseling, and if deans didn't make use of their research a new class of professionals with the dignified label of "Personnel Administrators" would.

By the 1930s what Harper had proposed as an ideal for the college community was cramping the dean's style. Dean Hawkes didn't like the way things were going any more than did his associates in the profession. "The personnel organization," he chided defensively, "cannot be centered in a separate office and carried on apart from the central administrative office of the institution. Im-

121

plicit in this philosophy of the interrelation of education and guidance is the theory that the office of the dean is the place where the personnel, as well as the academic policies of the college, should be planned and set into operation." [10]

Old-school professors thought students were better off if ignored and made to stand on their own two feet outside of classrooms. They grumbled about the expensive luxury of a dean, but they were more annoyed by the intrusion of psychologists trying to make a science out of counseling; they claimed that "prowling around in students' private affairs" was degenerating, nothing but "mollycoddling" and "wetnursing," that the "unwarranted interference" would weaken more students than it would help. And the deans themselves were not very receptive to the psychologists; they felt that they were doing a pretty good job without the assistance of impersonalized tests. They suspected how much the results could be trusted. Human qualities shouldn't be represented in terms of figures and formulae.

Scathingly the upstarts in the field of counseling dismissed what the old deans were doing as "sentimentalized intuition—ineffable and consequently above criticism," "parentalism mixed with common sense and good intentions."

The sniping went on for years with the deans outnumbered and the scientists steadily gaining ground, and it took World Wars I and II to bring a culmination to the tiff. The classification tests, the aptitude tests, the manpower charts, and the hundreds of psychological experiments used to determine service qualifications for millions of men offered dramatic evidence that a new technology and the IBM machine could be very useful in mass academic allocations. From the University of Minnesota, capital of the personnel philosophy, professionalism in testing human traits had swept into industry from coast to coast, into psychology departments, high schools, and even community organizations. And here and there trained specialists were moving into the deans' offices, replacing the amateurs with their "sentimentalized intuition."

Other forces were at work too. American education had always centered on the individual, but the multitude of postwar students, dispersed housing, substitution of auditoriums for classrooms, overburdened professors who could not possibly find time for consultation with individuals, and the very heterogeneity of students, were ruling out the old order. In the enormous universities something comparable to a production line had to help out with the counseling. The Minnesota system was the answer.

Where a dean was once "alone with God"—and seldom allowed many minutes in which to consult the Almighty— a well-buttressed director of personnel in a university of ten, twenty, or thirty thousand now had an echelon of specialists to whom he could refer his more complicated cases. There were expert counselors (with Ph.D.s) to handle every type of problem: financial counselors, religious counselors—Protestant, Catholic, and Jewish—dormitory counselors, fraternity counselors, student activities counselors, disciplinary counselors, marriage counselors, instructional counselors, vocational counselors, and if the guardians of the budget had really been sold on the crying need for an ample personnel program there was a staff of social workers to follow up a case, a medical clinic, psychiatrists and a therapeutic team, a corps of psychometrists, speech pathologists, and mental hygienists.

Fine departmental distinctions were made between vocational and personal counseling, between vocational counseling and short-term psychoanalytic treatment, between counseling and psychotherapy. And in a really progressive personnel setup a student didn't make an appointment with one of these experts for mere counseling: he went for "interview therapy."

A lad who could prove that he was thoroughly messed up and worthy of the plenary treatment would wind up having every lobe of his brain penetrated by the psychologists with aptitude, proficiency, and diagnostic tests: tests for native intelligence, educational achievement, and specialized ability; sensory perception and motor capacity; interest tests, personality tests, vocational and professional aptitude tests; and specific tests to determine mechanical aptitude, artistic aptitude, clerical aptitude.

In the background the experts, sparring for professional status and zealously protecting their departmentalization, engage in academic dispute over whether or not the campus psychiatric social case worker should practice psychotherapy, over the difference between the therapeutic techniques of the social worker and the psychiatrist, or the difference between the work of the psychiatric social case worker and other case workers. For their journals they write learned articles on distinctions between personnel counselors and personnel workers, between the directive and nondirective, counselor-centered and client-centered approaches. But somewhere in the labyrinth a troubled student can usually find the likeness of an old-fashioned dean who will talk over a prosy problem without benefit of psychoanalysis.

Despite all the streamlined organization designed to adjust the maladjusted, students with mighty good qualifications continue to flunk out of college. They represent the great tragedy in an inflexible system of higher education that ordinarily does not allow more than one try for a slow starter. Under unusual conditions an institution may readmit a one-time failure after a suitable moratorium, but too often he is through for keeps and no other self-respecting college is supposed to grant him sanctuary. The student fails, but the college also has failed—reluctant as its officials are to admit it—for the real fault may have been in the course advising, the living quarters, an all-too-attractive extracurricular program, an inadequate teaching staff, an inexcusable error of judgment in the admissions office, or, alas, yielding to the pressure tactics of an opulent alumnus to get him in.

Tens of thousands of these outcasts troop through the deans' offices every February and June, begging in desperation, in tears, in defiance for a second chance. They are put through the last counseling rites and referred to Uncle Sam or an employment office. For a few years there was something heroic about flunking out of college one week and patriotically slipping into a uniform the next, but that response has worn off. The dean undoubtedly is partly to blame for the student's failure, but when withdrawal time comes, as the official who issues the separation papers, he is likely to get *all* the blame. His colleagues on the faculty are under the impression that the standards of a college are lifted by arbitrary treatment of students who do not make good. And they have a point: academic standards are boosted, but it may be at very high cost to the individuals concerned.

Conscientious deans worry a great deal about the mounting casualty lists, the waste in educational effort, the waste in human resources, and the fact that the elaborate counseling programs have failed to cut down too appreciably on the appalling number of drops. A few of them recognize that serious effort to salvage the derelicts is one of the virtually unexplored major fields in higher education.

At least one clear-sighted institution, however, has taken a lead that might well have been grabbed by the professionals of the Harvard, Minnesota, or California class years ago. In defiance of the age-old tradition that it is detrimental to the principles and prestige of any accredited college to offer assistance to the flunks of a brother institution, Mitchell College at New London, Connecticut, in 1950 began to reserve a few places for men worthy of rehabilitation, and in less than a decade the faculty there have demonstrated beyond any doubt the error in abandoning first failures. By agreement with a dozen colleges, Mitchell volunteered each semester to take in some thirty or forty flunks nominated by their respective deans, to enroll them for a year or longer in courses comparable to those in which they had done unsatisfactory work, and, if they made good, to recommend their reinstatement at the original college.

The high proportion of successes was phenomenal. A

casualty from an Ivy League college, after a brief tour at Mitchell, went on for his doctorate at William and Mary. A student billed at Ohio Wesleyan as the Big Man of the Year, with a football captaincy, undergraduate government leadership, and a high place on the Dean's List to his credit, turned out to be a transfer from Mitchell previously dropped from another university. Of twenty men accepted from one Pennsylvania university over a period of two years, all but three returned to a senior college to make acceptable records.

"The typical rehabilitation student," as described by President Robert Weller of Mitchell, "is a very bright person. He has placed extracurricular activities, fraternities, and hobbies ahead of college. He can give only lip service to the values of a college education. He has little idea of the cost in effort of a quality degree from an accredited college. He evidences a good deal of latent hostility. He rarely knows very much about himself, his worth as a person and a student, or about where he is going in life. His needs have been well—too well—taken care of by society. Man-grown, he is still very much the child when it comes to responsibility."

That archetype bears a striking resemblance to the boys who have been paying the most frequent visits to the dean's office for a long time. When preliminary counseling doesn't bring them around, a moratorium may be in order. And the Mitchell variety of moratorium, offering a push rather than a penalty, may save a year and redirect a whole life. The courage and the charity to stake a man to a second chance is the humanitarian principle on which all remedial counseling is based.

Year by year the educational strategists are finding that their charts are less at variance. The professionals discover that they need the sensitive intuition of the humanitarians and the humanitarians discover that they need the scientific approach of the professionals. At divergent angles the two detachments are advancing toward a common goal. One day they will meet, join forces, and amicably proceed in unity.

6.

"MORE THAN AN ADMINISTRATOR, HE HAS TO BE AN ARTIST"

[*The Dean as Administrator*]

COLLEGES ARE as committee-conscious as a federation of women's clubs or the House of Representatives. Virtually every academic move is weighed in committee meetings of one sort or another, at levels stretching from the state legislature all the way down through the trustees, the administration, the faculty, and the student body to the latest arrivals in the freshman class. And since the dean has administrative obligations at all these levels —particularly the faculty level—his appointment calendar is lined and interlined with daily reminders of little assemblies which he is required to attend, or at which he is invited to testify.

The trouble with committees is mostly numerical, thinks Harvard sociologist Robert F. Bales, who has been studying them through a one-way mirror for almost a decade. He has decided the membership count shouldn't be over seven, and for top efficiency—four might be even better.[1]

But in academic circles there has always been a tendency to disregard Harvard exhortation—as well as to confuse the functions of a committee with the functions of a jury and a caucus, so the orthodox size of a policy-producing or law-levying faculty council stands at an unwieldy fifteen, and on a really vital matter, calling for the collaboration of a compact quartet, the total runs to thirty or forty. The larger the issue, the larger the committee: that's the rule of thumb.

The purpose of all this committee-mongering, according to the critics of committees, is to protect presidents and deans from any accusations of authoritarianism or incompetence, to spread the onus of unpopular rulings, to create a camouflage for someone to hide behind, and at the same time to foster the impression that the democratic ideal is all but running away with the show. The average dean of a decent-sized institution belongs to twenty-seven such tribunals. That certifies that he is a full-fledged administrator.

Around the oblong tables is considered every conceivable aspect of the educational community from curriculum to dormitory construction, from Johnny Doaks' readmission request to rebellious Henry Treeslip's whiskers. Decisions are made that will determine the addresses of ten thousand freshmen in 1970 and very seriously affect the future habitat of a single sophomore plagiarist before nightfall. Items on the agenda range from the resplendent to the ridiculous, from questions such as authorizing the appearance of a hell-fire revivalist to the pants worn by a campus existentialist.

When an upper New York university was threatened

with being turned into a winter nudist colony during a 1957 cold snap, trousers actually were the issue of debate for an emergency staff meeting. Assembled in academic dignity, the authors of university protocol had to decide whether or not there should be a law against freshmen making interdormitory dashes *en déshabillé*. It all started when a student picked up a twenty-five-dollar dare to make a midnight circuit of the campus in the nude and on the run, with the thermometer registering 23° below. The boy collected, and the freshman dormitory was in business. Others collected. Men given to inherent modesty didn't want to be excluded from the traffic, so for ten dollars they made the safari wearing G-strings. The campus radio station caught wind of the exposition, offered free air time, presented graphic accounts of the "chill–thrill" races, and castigated the student body for lack of college spirit in not coming out to root for the virile stars. Enthusiasts even thought of the possibilities in television.

Then the dormitory counselors cracked down. On the front steps they intercepted six pilgrims about to set forth attired in strings and suspenders. The troupers stoutly maintained that they were violating no college regulation; but the counselors ruled that indecent exposure was indecent exposure, so the half-dozen returned to their subscribers, had the bet changed to five dollars, and set forth in swimming trunks. At that point the fad had to be referred to the university dignitaries for a policy decision, and while they wagged their heads, the yearlings passed around the cough drops and waited in suspense. The confused debate over circumspection, "freedom with responsibility," jockstraps and pneumonia was still going on when a thaw fortuitously set in, and everybody lost interest in "chill–thrills."

A few miles farther north, Dean Frank Piskor at Syracuse enthusiastically accepted an appointment to a special faculty committee on Christmas decorations during the postwar veterans' period. In cooperation with New York State, an emergency housing area had been set up a considerable distance from the campus on an abandoned university farm, but the unlandscaped Quonset-hut village was bleak and barren, a depressing sight, when the first December snows blew into Syracuse. Someone had the bright idea of turning the village into a fairyland of lights and greenery for the holiday season. The Student Council came through with generous premiums for the most fetching decorations, and Dean Piskor, who was on the awards committee too, took considerable pride in presenting first prize to a unit lavishly festooned with a profusion of spruce boughs.

In the press the event was heralded as an esthetic triumph, the promoters and prizewinners honored. Christmas spirit was rampant. Everybody, or almost everybody, was happy about it. Expecting further encomium, the dean welcomed into his office the next day a distinguished delegation of public-spirited citizens who indicated that they had something to do with a nearby country club. But when they took their seats, he sensed that they were not in a holiday mood. One of the finest spruce trees on their golf course, a beautiful thirty-year-old specimen, seemed to be missing, they reported, and a telltale trail in the snow led directly from the fourth tee to the Quonset village. So Dean Piskor, who had so enthusiastically supported the decoration plan and so proudly announced the awards, found himself on still another committee to collect from impecunious veterans the sum of $600 for replacement of one evergreen.

The dean sits uneasily on short-term committees and long-term committees, on standing committees and subcommittees, but the permanent faculty committees are the ones that make him most restive. Take the typical student welfare committee that mediates on a multitude of major concerns like decorum, "exceptions," and proposals for alterations in the scripture of the undergraduate bible. This is the jury to which the dean, by faculty legislation, is required to submit cases and innovations that he is not authorized to settle alone—certain disciplinary dismissals, controversies overlapping two departments, clarifications of outmoded laws. To be sure, these items are peanuts compared to forty problems he takes care of by himself on any given day, but the faculty have no idea what a dean does, and assume that these are the momentous issues of the hour, to be considered with the gravity accorded a charter amendment.

The composition of this committee is subject to a great deal of faculty criticism, and before the bells ring in a new academic year, many hours of palaver have been spent in the presidential chambers on its make-up in an effort to forestall the critics. Since the president is expected to make student welfare his first concern, he assumes the chairmanship himself. (As the day for the monthly gathering approaches, however, he usually finds it necessary to take off on the alumni circuit, speak at a Rotary luncheon, or meet with a budget committee, so, in effect, the chairmanship actually falls to the senior officer present.) On the membership roster is a sprinkling of veeps and other deans, briefed to support the administrative party line on any controversial measures, but the main body of the committee is composed of free lances carefully chosen to represent (in minority) the dissident element and all the other elements of the faculty.

Counterclockwise around the table are the individualists: a member of the economics department who long ago gave up the law for pedagogy but who is still an authority on parliamentary order and much in demand among committeemen to resolve the procedural complications in which faculty people chronically entangle themselves; the precise professor of semantics who has a rare facility for elegantly restating motions or summarizing the main points of a prolix discussion without necessarily incorporating any of the purport of that discussion other than his own contributions; the hypochondriac who thinks the college is going to the dogs, says so, then doodles and dozes uncooperatively, or makes the most of the long periods of debate by drafting memos to subordinates in his department on matters he never can catch up on in his office; the associate professor with a private income who over the years has been shifted from one social science department to another but has always retained such a strong allegiance to athletics that he can tactfully redirect any discussion that infringes on the prerogatives of football, sailing, or quoits; the bored pedant who hates committees, raises an objection to every suggestion made, but does all the seconding, moves to table the most urgent matters

135

pending further study, and mercifully makes the motions for adjournment. (The last was a shot-in-the-dark appointment, a badly calculated risk. He never serves on a committee longer than one year, yet there will be another like him to take his place next season.)

Then there are three very important plants on the committee: a representative of the senior contingent of the faculty, a representative of the juniors, and an odd figure whom everyone recognizes as an independent. The senior, aged sixty-two, has been seated with the same committee since he was thirty-two and hasn't altered his concept of educational administration in the interim. Out of the deference to old age, no one expresses, orally, any objection to his qualifications for membership, though his principal contribution is prolongation of the proceedings through supplying "perspective," introducing irrelevant instances of student behavior of the past, cautioning against hasty decisions, and presenting a new angle just as some trifling matter is coming to a vote. In his long tenure on the committee he has never been known to commit himself aggressively, say, to the extent of actually phrasing a motion, though on many occasions he has repeated paraphrastically exactly what the chairman has just said as if it were an inspiration.

At the foot of the table sits the junior faculty representative, to whom, again, no one can take exception out of deference to his youth. "It is well to get the newcomers interested early," says the president; this choice is particularly felicitous, for the instructor is obviously striking for a department chairmanship, and in less than two years is known to have entertained the president and his wife for dinner at least thrice. He can be counted on to withhold any personal convictions in favor of what is best for the long-range benefit of the college and the shorter-range advancement of his chief executive. His remarks are directed only to the chair or to a sympathetic vice-president halfway up the table.

Alongside the junior sits the last member, a middle-aged chemist who has been marvelously shielded from the sins of the world. He is soft-spoken, methodical, slow to wrath, and unconsciously expresses his embarrassment over any case involving sex by flushing a deep crimson; he tends to giggle when perplexed and fails to crack a smile at the sociologist's off-color wisdom; rarely does he make any comment at all, but once or twice a year he bursts forth in an unpredictable tirade of indignation on a subject that everyone assumed was furthest removed from his interests. That spark of fire keeps him on the committee. The way his vote will gravitate is a tossup.

At such a gathering comes up the question of what special consideration can be given the stellar basketball center who has just failed his fourth midyear exam, the enigma of repeated parking violations on the part of students who are merely following the example set by estimable faculty members, the question of whether or not to permit a senior to graduate after trying unsuccessfully for four years to pass the required freshman swimming test although he has ably met all other requirements for a degree, the problem of Gamma Kappa Rho, which made a shambles of the Roaring Brook Pavilion last week end during their spring formal—a problem complicated by the common knowledge that three influential trustees happen to be Gamma Kappas and one of them chaperoned the party. Decisions are rarely unanimous, and the altercations stirred up in the meetings carry over into private life, establish permanent feuds among faculty wives, seep down to student levels, and help to keep the campus in ferment when all other schisms are mended.

Dr. Bales advises that a good committee should be "seeded" with two star performers: "the task leader" and "the social leader"—the task leader being the go-getter who supplies the bright ideas, irritates everyone, challenges old prejudices, and keeps things moving, while his more popular partner, the pacifist and suave mediator, is engaged in "mending the fences and rubbing arnica on the bruised toes." But in their eagerness to get democratic action and collateral support, the administrators who align faculty committees disregard this advice too, and overdo things by indiscriminate seeding of leaders, with the result that there is too much germination, inadequate tillage and irrigation, some unfortunate cross-fertilization, a great many hybrid compromises, and a harvest of brand-new problems to keep subcommittees busy for another year.

The dean fits into this group admirably, is indistinguishable from the others, ducks issues, and doodles with the best of them. But he does it with a difference, for he is the administrator. Their picnic is his purgatory. As the group swings toward another unrealistic compromise, he sees himself in the ambiguous position of having to execute a mandate totally in conflict with his own best judgment. He is particularly good on the small, manageable subcommittee which can be persuaded to report "progress" periodically—until the parent committee has forgotten the nature of the original assignment.

Dean Scott Goodnight of Wisconsin favored the abortive subcommittee, which he described as a "body appointed to see that nothing is done." "If the chairman proves to be a conscientious soul," Goodnight elucidated, "he will call the committee together and the result will be a report. This report will be duly reported to the parent body and eventually discussed and approved by it. Then the report will be carefully filed away, wrapped in excelsior, with moth balls, and everybody is happy. The committee has done its duty and been honorably discharged; its conscience is clear, and the *corpus delicti* is cheerfully interred where it will *requiescat in pace* until the judgment day." [2]

Such estimable workmanship, however, is extremely rare. Far more common are the dedicated bench warmers who develop into a kind of junta, see in their effort the only possible salvation for the institution, seize upon their appointment as an opportunity to vent their favorite peeves, and, as a University of California observer sardonically suggests, "a committee appointed to see that chalk is furnished to all blackboards turns in a report which demands a new president or an extra year in the curriculum." [3]

Deans are cynical about outsized, busybody committees. They complain that so much time is spent in them deciding what to do that there is no time left to do it. By profession they are whipping boys anyway, and they resent the additional umbrage of being classified as "committee whipping boys." They hate long-drawn-out, cantankerous meetings, but they are also suspicious of meetings that run too smoothly: too much agreement is as clear a sign of trouble as too much disagreement. They'd like to see committees torn down once a year, given a period of self-study, and made to justify their existence. They realize that the original purpose for the appointment of a college committee was sound: it was designed to do away with the evils of both dictatorship and cumbersome democracy by substituting a limited oligarchy. The idea was to toy with a problem and come up with a wiser answer than any one person could make, a synthesis better than the sum of all the ideas aired. But that concept was short-lived. More than a century ago a Columbia scholar returned from a frustrating committee session to jot in his diary: "Most imbecile Columbia College meeting this afternoon. Literally nothing accomplished." [4] It's an old game.

A very large part of the dean's endeavor labeled "administration" isn't administration at all; it's a verbal endurance race around the oblong table. Basically, of course, he's an autocrat, unreceptive to other people's solutions. He likes to get things done—his way, the best way, without so much thrashing about. Life would be far less complex if only Dr. Bales' creed on quartets, or even septets, would be harkened unto. The dean is certain that a committee of four or five could reach just as sound a decision as twenty-five on what to do about Henry Treeslip's whiskers or the ten thousand freshmen expected in 1970. Moreover, policy recommendations have to go to the faculty for ultimate approval anyway. Is a brainwashing caucus really necessary?

Since the dean's responsibilities overlap the responsibilities of everyone else in the college community, administrative progress for him is inevitably dependent on expeditious exchange of sentiment. But bench-warming on faculty committees—and almost as many student committees—is only one phase of his job as administrator. He is forever in and out of the president's office, the comptroller's office, the registrar's office, and all the other offices. He is drafting plans for better supervision of residence halls, explaining to alumni associations the need for a change in the old athletic scholarship program, persuading the purchasing agent that the beds designed for the projected dormitory should be six inches longer because students come more elongated than they used to, giving a reporter a different slant to the story on last night's dormitory riot by substituting facts for impressions.

In the outer office a formidable number of visitors and inquisitors are waiting to see him "just for a minute" that turns into an hour and a half. Representatives from all the investigative agencies in the country, for instance, descend upon him one by one in their collective campaign to purge the nation of subversive influences. The quidnunc from the State Department wants an unequivocal statement that Absalom Shinburn, '49, applicant for a job as courier to the Antipodes, never indulged in any off-color shenanigans on the campus. The FBI begs to see a copy of the constitution of the Reformers Club which Jimmy Startup, '57, candidate for a "highly confidential government position," was naïve enough to admit on his personal history declaration he once belonged to. Intelligence sleuths from the Navy, the Army, and the Air Force, Civil Service investigators, cloak-and-dagger operatives from far-off cities make pryingly personal inquiries, and then, as if doubting the official word, prowl around among the faculty to assess the dean's reliability as a character witness.

As late as the 1920s a few failures and a reputation as a vigorous college cutup were virtually essential to a student trying to land a position with a well-bred investment banking firm, but all that has changed in the new public concern with "records"—and details omitted from the records which the dean may obligingly recall. The privacy once associated with affairs that went on behind college walls is no more. Public, press, and government agents are convinced that they have a right to the inside information, and they know where to go for it.

An imperturbable dean was forced to halt his other administrative duties for days while his office swarmed with FBI agents, postal inspectors, VA officials, state troopers, local cops and lawyers, all exercising their prerogatives of probing into the affairs of a single junior-class member. Through a little investigation of his own, the dean had discovered that Bill Barkley had an overwhelming aversion to examinations. A single slippery excuse started him off, and one thing led to another in rapid succession. To avoid the ordeal of taking tests at the assigned time and place, the young prevaricator would resort to any subterfuge. Over a period of three years he had "accidentally" fallen out of a third-story dormitory window on the eve of a course reckoning, had faked an automobile accident on another occasion, at the critical hour involved himself as an informant in an unsolved murder case, feigned sudden illness as he entered the examination room, cleverly forged the registration stamp of the U.S. mail in returning a test taken at home, inflicted painful wounds upon himself as a dodge for surrendering to his examiners, repeatedly talked professors into letting him write finals in his room, in the library, in hospitals, anywhere monitors would be careless and cooperative about leaving reference notes within reach.

One by one the instances had come to light as the dean delved into the past, and the record for fraud in taking examinations was only a point of departure for the trails of improbity which the investigative agents wanted to follow. Fact was, Bill Barkley in three years had never taken a written quiz of any consequence under normal circumstances, yet he was ranked as an outstanding student and recognized campus leader. He had been so disarming, so diabolically clever in his machinations that no faculty member ever held him under suspicion until the truth began to leak out, and even then professors were more of a pest to the dean than the retinue of detectives; they still couldn't believe Bill was capable of committing an indiscretion and wanted to rescue him from the inclemency of a vindictive dean.

Bill, incidentally, found temporary refuge in a psychiatric ward, then talked his way out of that predicament and into another college where, just before final examinations, he was incapacitated by an accidental jamming of his writing fingers under the lid of a trunk.

Administratively the dean remains in the middle—the bridge between the faculty and the students, between the students and the staff, between the students, the staff, and intruding outsiders. He is supposed to interpret to students the policies adopted by higher authority, and convey to his superiors the reactions of the students, meantime preserving among his charges a nice balance between freedom and responsibility. And when the wires in his implicated network of communication get crossed, all hell breaks loose.

"The administration has had a simple formula for the dean of students," commented Robert Strozier on his tenth anniversary in that position at the University of Chicago. "It established the office to represent services of all kinds, except curricular and strictly business. To their somewhat amorphous structure has been added, through the years, anything which the administration considered vexing. Obviously the dean of students is to blame if anything goes wrong. The sweet reasonableness of the administration's position is mute testimony to the clarity of thinking along administrative lines: 'Bob, that's a lousy editorial in the *Maroon* this morning'; 'Well, I see the students have a pipe-line to the Council of the Senate'; 'Why do our students always have to be different?'; 'Why should we be accused of discrimination? Look around you'; 'More money for student aid? Don't you know there's a deficit?'; 'A trustee's name was left out of the directory, you know'; 'Why can't we publish a catalogue which can be understood?'; 'Tell us exactly what the enrollment will be next year, five years, ten years from now'—all routine questions." [5]

A new university president fresh from the business world and comfortably unenlightened on what his dean did in the big office at the end of the corridor, was anxious to keep him interested in affairs of the academic family, so almost daily he obligingly sent down a new batch of busywork. Afraid that he might embarrass the dean with prying inquries about how he spent his time, the president delayed a formal reckoning until the dean began complaining of ulcers, and, with an air that hinted of resignation, appealed for a statement of exactly what was expected of him.

"Perhaps you would start off by giving me a résumé of the areas in which you already carry responsibilities," countered the president considerately, but a little miffed.

The dean came back with a detailed list next day. It included such items as freshman orientation; maintenance of thousands of personnel records; supervision of counseling services, health services, remedial study services, housing and food services; superintendence of extracurricular and recreational activities; handling of all disciplinary cases; managing a financial aid and student employment program; organizing a placement bureau; advising foreign students; integrating a religious activities program; offering free counsel to married students on everything from family budgets to birth control—and serving on some two dozen committees.

The president ran his pencil down the list incredulously, asked a few penetrating questions, solemnly went over it a second and a third time in an unsuccessful attempt to eliminate something, and finally concluded in awe: "You need some more assistants, don't you!" The dean got three and received no more assignments in busywork.

"We are entering upon a period when of necessity our institutions shall be forced to accommodate students in greater and greater numbers with relatively fewer and fewer teaching and administrative personnel," declared

145

Dean John E. Hocutt of the University of Delaware. "Some persons have predicted that over the next ten years or so there will be a shift completely away from the concept of the individual. If our efforts are to benefit any appreciable number of students, there must be a greater emphasis upon administration—a more effective budgeting of time and skills, more care paid to delegating, and more skillful relating of the parts to the whole. Working in an increasingly complex and demanding situation, the dean, as administrator, and his effectiveness depend upon his skill in working with and through a growing staff of specialists."[6]

In the giant streamlined education factories the day of "greater emphasis upon administration" has already arrived. The dean is a big operator, an administrator with a capital *A*, spending far more time in consultation with his colleagues than in consoling individual undergraduates, and even then he complains that he is kept so busy pumping water out of the flooded basement that he doesn't have time to go upstairs and repair the leaky plumbing.

Dr. W. H. Cowley, Professor of Education at Stanford, and a lifetime student of the evolution of educational supervision, sees the humanitarians who comprised the "first wave" of student personnel administrators dying off, and, taking their places, a "second wave" recruited for their administrative ability rather than for any "compelling interest in students or in student life"—"executives in charge of large and important operations." Addressing a group of them, he charged, "You are the top dogs of the enterprise. You deal with the presidents and academic deans; you wrangle the budget; you direct the work of staffs that steadily increase in size; but generally you are too busy to talk with students other than the presidents of student organizations and those in serious trouble with the administration." [7]

Perhaps that is an exaggeration, for even the most professional administrator can be an approachable, humanitarian dean, and, if he doesn't answer the description, lurking around in the background somewhere there is bound to be a subordinate whom the students recognize as the real thing. The top dogs in the great universities are usually "Deans of Students," "Directors of Student Personnel," or "Vice Presidents" in charge of a corps of underlings, including the dean of men and the dean of women. The setup hints of a superimposed bureaucracy, isolated and imperious, but any such assumption is in error; a successful dean's office is always in servitude to the rest of the institution.

Taking refuge in the confines of a department is one of the academic privileges denied the dean. He represents no segment. His is an interdepartmental post, spanning both the curricular and the extracurricular limits. He cannot make fine distinctions between classroom learning and education acquired in the social laboratories of the Student Union, a fraternity house, or the gymnasium. Administratively he has to be concerned with creating an environment and an undergraduate morale conducive to edification. He agrees with Professor Gilbert Wrenn of Minnesota who maintains that "laboratories for living are as important as properly equipped science laboratories and art studios." [8]

For the dean, the athletic and social programs, the dormitory and dining-hall environment, the physical setting

147

of the campus and all the administrative offices are integral parts of the instructional blueprint. Even the offices conducting the business affairs of a college—those most frequently considered farthest removed from the teaching faculty—have to fit into this instructional pattern, and at least one representative from that contingent, the treasurer of Purdue, Dr. Robert B. Stewart acknowledges it forcefully. "Business officers are educators," he says, "and they are among the most important educators in higher education, if they understand their function, which is helping young people develop and find themselves in life; but they have to do it without letting the student know he is being taught. And this requires the highest type of reaching there is. . . . By directing environment we create in the student the desire to be what the faculty and so-called educators and the rest of us think he ought to be. The student therefore educates himself through our efforts and this is the prime purpose for which we are running an institution." [9]

The English system of higher education, suggests California's President Clark Kerr, offers a protected life for "a well-integrated member of a particular social class"; the German system "offers a fragmentary environment, channeled toward the vocational life, and forms an occupational servant of the state"; but America has committed itself to recognition of the "total student," by providing "a complete and diversified environment," designed to influence "the whole life of the student and to form a responsible citizen of a democracy." [10]

Another college executive, Victor Spathelf, President of Ferris Institute in Michigan, who came up through the ranks as dean at Wayne University, aptly summarizes the philosophy: "The modern student personnel program is not an isolated or segregated patrol activity apart from the main task force of the college's educational resources. . . . It becomes the means of introducing the student to himself in a new environment, and the student is a different person in this new environment, believe it or not, for good or for evil. . . . It is the agent of the college for removing the obstacles to effective learning, whether these be physical or spiritual, psychological or material things. It is the seeker-outer of those who become lost in the academic process, and there are a lot of them that become lost. . . . It is the institution's morale builder, as it assists in group identification, and as it assists in personal identification. . . . This modern program should be the prime coordinator of the learning experiences which employ both the classroom and the extra-classroom activities. . . . It is a program which must deal intimately with the mental and emotional, and the spiritual and economic, social, cultural and recreative phases of a student's life, not as a meddler performs, not as a drooling, over-enthusiastic helper, not as a starry-eyed reformer, but as a wise teacher and counselor . . . and the person who directs that program has to be more than an administrator; he has to be an artist as well, an artist devoted to creative thinking and creative operation." [11]

Such a program passes on to students more responsibility than they have ever held before, and as crash plans for accommodations of doubled enrollments materialize during the next decade, undergraduates will be getting a larger and larger share in college operations—exactly what they have been requesting for a long time. The shift is already under way. With competence and self-reliance, they serve as their own legislators, judges, and residence-hall managers. They operate their own courts and mete out penalties which offenders accept without too much ill will—though here deans see danger signals, for with the abdication of responsibility for discipline goes an important counseling opportunity. In a few institutions students are even represented on the highest faculty tribunals and on governing boards of trustees. Pretty generally administrators have followed the stand taken by Dr. Strozier that "we should not *direct* student activities; rather we should encourage and support them, allowing the students themselves to gain real educational experience from organizing a rich and varied extracurriculum." [12]

The distribution of details at least helps to clear the dean's desk so that he can be free for consultation when the real posers bob up. The dean of students at a southwestern university was congratulating himself on how smoothly twelve thousand undergraduates were taking to the orientation and registration program during the opening days of the new academic year; his desk was unlittered; his assistants were functioning smoothly; he had delegated so many responsibilities he was beginning to wonder if perhaps he shouldn't reclaim some of the duties he had passed off.

Then, suddenly, as happens in every dean's office periodically, the telephone started ringing; the press, the public, and the president were upon him; a dozen emergencies came at once, and he had to take care of them all *personally.* There was no delegating of such matters. A student, whose admission to the infirmary had allegedly been delayed in the confusion of an Asiatic flu epidemic, died tragically, bringing the wrath of parents, an influential fraternity, and the student body upon the dean's office. As he was starting investigations of that casualty, the report came in from the police that a despondent freshman had driven to an isolated spot two miles from town, left farewell notes in his car addressed to his parents and a girl friend, and shot himself.

While trying to get in touch with bereft parents, an urgent message arrived from the health service explaining that twenty-eight more cases of flu had just been admitted to the infirmary, bringing the total to over five hundred, and additional space for wards would have to be found somewhere without delay. Simultaneously a vial labeled *Nitroglycerine* turned up in the attic of a fraternity house—enough to demolish the structure; police and demolition experts had to be summoned, and by the time they had heroically disposed of the bottle, the whole affair was being laughed off by its perpetrators as a pleasant hoax.

The student senate chose that day to decide that the university had been most inconsiderate in ending the Christmas holidays on January 2. Looking ahead three months, they foresaw that they would be missing out on all the New Year's parties at home, and wanted the administration to take prompt action in amending the calendar—never guessing how such a change could upset hundreds of class schedules, not to mention professorial engagements already made, or the curricular, laboratory,

151

dining-hall, and repair-crew programs which have to be slated far in advance.

All this served as a fair prelude for still more of what deans call "devastating diversity." The report of a co-ed stabbing came next, and a newspaper reporter, convinced that the dean was trying to shield the university from further adverse publicity, was ready to go to press with all the blood-stained details when the truth was finally tracked down: the stabbing was a faked assault staged by law students for a mock trial.

But there was nothing spurious about the delicate problem waiting in the dean's outer office while the reporters were being assuaged. A brainy, seventeen-year-old transfer had been rolled. Yes, he responded to the dean's cross-examination, it was in a joy house; he'd been there on several occasions, but he had learned his lesson and was ready to reform. So he produced the straight facts, and with artful intervention on the part of the dean, a paddy wagon was soon in service, resulting in the booking of eight prostitutes and assorted customers. And before the dust was settling from these events, the dean was mediating a pregame ruckus in a host city involving thousands of students, unfortunate casualties, offended police, concerned parents, irate citizens, and ravenous newspaper correspondents.

Fortunately there wasn't a single undergraduate mental crack-up during that whole sequence. They usually come later in the year in the midst of other seasonal convulsions. The prize episode to fit that category belongs to Indiana University, where Jerry Dyer steamed into the dean's office one morning to break the news to Assistant

Dean Leo Dowling that something was wrong with his head; he was afraid he was going off his rocker.

"Is that so!" sympathized the assistant. "Any special symptoms?"

"Yes," replied Jerry mysteriously. "Every time I open my dresser drawer at my rooming house I see pancakes."

Dowling admitted that a situation like that was odd, but he took the disclosure in stride and decided that any boy who saw pancakes where pajamas ought to be was entitled to assume he was mentally distraught. They talked for a while and Jerry quite happily accepted the advice that it might be well to discuss the matter with a counselor.

But a week or two later Jerry showed up again to explain that while the counselor was proving to be very helpful and he felt he was getting better, he still occasionally saw pancakes in his dresser drawer. The assistant dean thought it advisable to brief his boss, Dean Robert Shaffer, on the case at this point, and after a protracted conference the two concluded that the boy undoubtedly had a problem and should consult the psychiatrist.

Jerry obligingly went off to the psychiatrist. Weeks passed. The incident was closed and almost forgotten in the dean's office when once more Jerry appeared, this time wringing his hands and in an emotionally desperate state. He was more troubled than ever by the same illusion.

"It was then," says Dowling, "that I made a momentous decision, and a fairly obvious one. I accompanied the student to his room, marched in to show him for himself that he was entertaining a sheer fantasy. I opened the dresser

153

drawer as proof, and there, interlarded with sheets, shirts, and unlaundered socks, I tell you, I never saw so damn many pancakes in all my life." [13]

Sometimes the administrating dean feels far removed from the realm of artistry.

7.

"THERE MUST BE JUDGES, POLICE-MEN, HANGMEN AND DEANS"

[The Dean as Disciplinarian]

"A DEAN who is not a good policeman soon loses his job," confessed an anonymous incumbent in a popular magazine article during the roaring '20s. "Ideally considered," he elaborated, "a dean is a guide-philosopher-and-friend for the young under his charge, the person to whom they bring their troubles of every kind—scholastic, financial, amatory, and moral—a man of wide experience, mellow wisdom, and youthful heart, to whom young men will freely unbosom, and who will understand as father would—or should. . . . But actually no college in these days lets its dean be such a counselor, except incidentally, and almost unofficially. Practically he is a policeman. He must spend substantially all his time promulgating, and, so far as possible, enforcing, the multifarious rules and regulations which the faculty are constantly enacting. Among the things which it is the dean's business to make the students do are the following:

1. To spend, spasmodically at least, a certain minimum of time in study.
2. To attend classes.
3. To attend chapel.
4. To participate in military drill.
5. To take regular exercise.
6. To be vaccinated.
7. To refrain from gross cheating in (a) final examinations, (b) midsemester quizzes, (c) laboratory exercises, and (d) themes, theses, and other written work prepared outside the classroom.
8. To refrain from getting drunk, at least in public.
9. To refrain from smoking in college buildings.
10. To keep hazing and class scraps within such bounds that actual loss of life or limb will not occur frequently.
11. To omit from college comic magazines jokes or pictures of such undisguised indecency as would render the publication unmailable under U. S. postal regulations.
12. To close college dances at some specified hour prior to daybreak.
13. To have at least nominal chaperones present at such dances.
14. To pay their bills to the college and local merchants.
15. To refrain from writing checks with no balance in the bank; also from forgery.
16. To refrain from using automobiles except under certain narrow restrictions.
17. To keep off the grass." [1]

The best interests of the profession have not always been served by public acknowledgment of what its agents are up to, but that anonymous testimonial let the cat out of the bag, and thereafter deans were obliged to carry their night sticks more openly.

In the three intervening decades the mortarboard cops have tried assiduously to disguise their operations under ornate euphemisms and flossy lingo borrowed from the psych department, but there has been no appreciable change in their beat. The compulsion has gone out of most of the daily chapel services which for generations were an effective form of group counseling; the smoking lamp has been lighted in many a classroom; scores of comic magazines have died unnatural and painful deaths; cars have been so freely admitted to the campus that only dignity forbids the erection of a row of gas pumps north of the library; yet deans are still preoccupied with keeping students from abusing their cutting privileges, keeping them from cheating and running riot, keeping them off the grass. If it weren't for the police duties, deans would have been invited to shut up shop before this—and that in spite of the refined glossary which has been invented to describe what they are doing. Remove the sins and shortcomings of undergraduates and there would be no need for an enforcement officer; students would run their own affairs, and professors would stampede to accept honors as club advisers and advocates.

Law enforcement, of course, is a distasteful academic occupation and when the psychologists discovered that counseling and disciplining should not be indulged in by one and the same person, the more opportunistic deans, calling themselves personnel administrators, were quick to seize upon the discovery as an out: it was humiliating for any high-powered counselor to be a disciplinarian, so another hireling was nominated to do the police work and it became fashionable in higher education for a really efficient operator to profess complete ignorance of all techniques that had anything to do with compulsion or repression.

For years the educational journals were heavy with verbiage belauding the fortunate divorce. Counseling, declared the progressive practitioners, was a "growth-producing," "ego-strengthening," "self-regulatory," "affect-integrating" art; it was highly personal and confidential, "self-initiated" and "self-centered," and the men who dedicated themselves to that art should avoid at all costs imposing any kind of restriction or punishment; they must remain "neutral." The miscreant was a favored individual to be approached without authoritarianism or threat, in order that he might be more agreeable to the acceptance of an inviting course of rehabilitation. Disciplining, on the other hand, was a form of punitive "force-control"—repressive, regulatory, bound to produce resentment; it was concerned exclusively with law and orderliness (and often "drum-head justice"). Instead of being personal and confidential, it was a "public" matter involving conformity to "societal demands."

Tommyrot! said the old-timers. The dean has to serve *in loco parentis.* No self-respecting father would make such distinctions. Counseling and disciplining are one and the same thing. "In recent years," declared an irritated partisan, Dean Edward Durnall of Nasson College,

158

"enough intellectual gibberish has been written on the topic of discipline to build a bridge of paper pulp from here to Peter Pan's 'Never-Never Land.' From reading most of the gobbledegook one gets the impression that the authors are still terrified of Captain Hook and that they take their own Winnie the Poohs to bed with them each night to protect themselves from the boogie man they have created. . . . Discipline is not bad, unnatural, conducive to frustration, ego-damaging, or repressive. The correct definition of discipline is training which corrects, molds, strengthens, and perfects. . . . Learning is impossible without discipline. . . . Students do not reject discipline as such unless they have been conditioned to do so. . . . Most individuals recognize the need for discipline and many are uncomfortable without it. The counselor must recognize that the individual who is in need of discipline is in no way different from the counselee who evidences other problems of adjustment." [2]

This war between the counselors and the disciplinarians still rages; the lines are drawn and the embattled forces take frequent pot shots at one another, but there are signs of confusion in the ranks. Some of the more ardent progressives at last are admitting that the ultimate aims of counseling and the ultimate aims of the disciplinarians aren't entirely divergent; their weaseling goes so far as to imply that the counselor may wish to compromise his neutrality and let the student know that he is "on the side of morality and law." Guardedly they explain that situations may arise in which compulsion is called for, "but we must not deceive ourselves that we are using an educational method." [3]

Occasionally they admit that the disciplinarian, too, has rehabilitation in mind, that the counselor does not hold a monopoly in dispersing "growth-producing" guidance, that he has to be concerned with the client's "public relations" as well as individuality. It is altogether possible that an armistice may eventually be declared. Meantime the small-college deans, who constitute the majority in the profession, continue their Janus-headed duties, and don't find too much inconsistency in the old- or new-fashioned dual role.

The supreme disadvantage in being either the faculty police agent or the student culprit is the lack of definition on the special dispensations to which a college student is entitled. The world over, students have always had dispensations—perhaps for no good reason. The kind of cheating that might bring a sophomore a fatherly reprimand would, in the business world, be enough to put a dishonest clerk of the same age bracket behind bars. Such harsh terms as larceny or robbery were rarely applied to the chicken-snatching of the 1890s, nor are they to the sign-lifting of the 1950s. A nightly pestilence of hullabalooing on a campus can be dismissed lightly as an expression of "youthful exuberance," but anywhere else it would be cause for mass incarceration as a deliberate affront to the peace and dignity of the state. Students have been getting away with it for centuries—to the chagrin of their lay brothers who go to jail for similar offenses, and deans are guilty of helping to perpetuate the tradition.

The happy award of martyrdom went to an undergraduate agitator who set up his soap box on a downtown street corner, inflamed his audience into a mood of riot with vituperative haranguing against local politicians, and finally submitted uncooperatively to arrest after ignoring repeated requests from police officers to dismiss his gathering. Charged with disorderly conduct, he was taken into court and declared guilty. Even then the privileged student wasn't ready to take such abuse; his case went all the way to the New York Supreme Court before he accepted defeat. But a distinguished educator put in the last word for him: "What we wonder," he protested softly, "is whether, when students' misdeameanors occur outside the campus jurisdiction, the interests of society and the students might not be more adequately served if civil officials consulted with college deans before charges are preferred. . . . This policy could (1) reduce the chances of student offenders acquiring police records that might affect them adversely later on; (2) relieve already overcrowded court calendars; (3) save public moneys; (4) most important, place remedial action in the hands of those who know the students best." [4]

As long as the double standard in law enforcement exists, deans will continue to take advantage of it for the benefit of their clientele; after all, it is the only humane procedure, though there would be more justice in the practice if similar privileges were accorded noncollege youth. Ironically enough, undergraduates usually have far more terror of the arm of college law than of local law, and with good reason, for a few days behind bars or a fifty-dollar fine is modest penalty compared to delaying a professional career several semesters or forfeiting it entirely due to premature separation from classes. But in an effort to offer a little better education in legal perspective, careful town-gown delimitation agreements have been drafted in most college communities and some of the equivocation on the due process of law eliminated.

"There must be judges, policemen, hangmen and deans," [5] Princeton's Dean Gauss allowed, but he didn't approve of the punitive approach any more than did many of his contemporaries—any more than do their soft-hearted successors. He granted that punishment was sometimes defensible from the social viewpoint, necessary for the good of the community, but it was the lazy way of solving problems, justifiable only when it would have a corrective, awakening effect upon both the individual and the group. That conviction is still shared by present-day disciplinarians: punishment without restoration is the shoddiest of treatment.

Bringing conventional order to the campus is doubly complicated by the topsy-turvy code of behavior that collegians automatically adopt upon matriculation. Reverence for personal ownership is surrendered. Life in a dormitory or fraternity house is communal, with everything from neckties to lecture notes, mattresses to automobiles more or less communalized. Temporary appropriation of another's property without consent is frowned upon but by no stretch of the imagination regarded as thievery. There is no such thing as privacy. Putting up with the idiosyncrasies, disturbances, and constant interruptions of neighbors is taken for granted. Traditional standards of right and wrong are freely abandoned, and current moral shortcomings of the world at large are accepted as the prevailing mores. The individual takes refuge in the group, and finding strength and concurrence in numbers, a student body proceeds to inflict its custom-built conventions on the college authorities and an unappreciative public.

Five hundred milling students descend upon a local movie theater, sweep past the box office, the protesting manager, a helpless police officer, and appropriate every seat in the auditorium. The manager could turn on the lights and stop the show, but he knows he could pay heavily for it in the ruckus that would follow immediately and in the boycott that would come later. Better to accept the invasion in good spirit as one of the perils of operating a theater in a college town. It happens periodically at every seat of higher learning.

Between the halves of a football classic a block of bibulous undergraduates decide it would be fun to provide a little interference for the intricate formations of the opponent's flashy band. They weave in and out of the lines with such amusing results that hundreds more want to get in on the demonstration. Chaos ensues. With the band disbanded, the magnificent drum becomes an object of conquest, trombones become effective weapons in the joust, and a real brawl is born. Clarinets are broken on the hard pates of sophomore attackers, oboes orbited around the necks of freshmen. And when it's all over, the wounds healed, the mutilated instruments paid for, shocked alumni placated, no one has the faintest idea of why it all started in the first place.

"Haven't had so much fun since I've been in college," was the consensus even of upperclassmen at Berkeley, California, about ten o'clock on the evening of May 16, 1956. Off and on for five hours thousands of University

163

of California students—men and women—had been dousing each other with water from hoses, hydrants, buckets, wastepaper baskets, paper bags, balloons, and old tin cans. They had given the police a hard time, too; in fact things were so out of hand early in the evening that city officers had put up roadblocks to detour traffic around the battle zones to protect outsiders from getting sloshed —all of which the water warriors appreciated, for they assumed that the police were merely setting aside the area as a sort of playground, and placing their blessings on the fun the scholars were having. It was a hot, humid evening; anyone interested in getting wetted down had taken advantage of the proceedings by ten o'clock; the crowds disbanded, the streetblocks were removed, and most of the officers went back to their regular duties.

But the water fights were only the preliminary romp for much more to come. The emotional hangover erupted into a panty raid that was chronicled around the world. "Screaming girls were carried through the streets naked, after 3000 rioting men students invaded their college dormitories last night," yowled the London *Daily Mirror,* as if a Rape of the Sabines were being reenacted in the United States. "The men at the University were staging a 'pantie raid.' Yelling and screaming they charged into the girls' bedrooms, beating up girls who attempted resistance. Beds were overturned, bedding hurled out of windows, furniture wrecked, and doors torn off hinges. Several girls had their pajamas torn off and were carried shoulder high into the streets."

The further the story traveled from the scene, the more embroidered it became. Actually there was no personal

164

violence, no disrobing of co-eds, no carting around of conquests in the raw or in pajamas. A horrified undergraduate, writing from hearsay for the University daily, started the rumors by reporting erroneously that "A few girls who dared face the mob with hot irons, paddles, or table lamps, were knocked around, assaulted, carried outside in pajamas or nude," and the fiction built up from there. Nevertheless, the rioters, moving from dormitories to sororities to rooming houses and back to dormitories, climbing into windows, ascending fire escapes, pouring into back doors and front, managed to purloin 1073 pieces of lingerie and other clothing; they appropriated personal effects valued at over $7000, and damaged residence-hall property to the extent of over $5000. [6]

When the hysteria had worn off, the most ardent participants were appalled at the wreckage they had wrought, at the ill repute they had brought upon themselves, and upon American education in general; the abandon merely highlighted a series of similar raids that had been taking place at universities like Minnesota, Pennsylvania, Northwestern, Harvard, Yale, Columbia, Wisconsin, Stanford, UCLA, Kansas, and Brigham Young.

"Such an affair is bad for all colleges and universities, not merely for the one where it occurs," scolded Dr. Austin H. MacCormick, a criminologist who had dealt with more prison riots than any living American. "The attitude toward serious student misconduct, individual or group, will strengthen or weaken the opinion of millions of people who already think that college and university administrators and faculties are complacently tolerant of reck-

165

less and even lawless conduct on the part of students, that we do not insist that they grow up, that we indirectly, if not directly, encourage a sense of special license to be irresponsible. . . . The most sinister aspect of delinquency today is the aggressive, violent, at times sadistically cruel behavior in which large numbers of juveniles and youths are involved—'wolf packs' and 'rat packs' beating small boys, legless veterans, and harmless old ladies into unconsciousness. . . . Mass misconduct on the part of people who should know better—all the way from strikers armed with lead pipes to a student mob—helps to set the pattern of behavior for underprivileged youths. . . . A mob of any type or composition is an ugly and terrifying thing. If I had the responsibility and power, I would bring a mob under control at the earliest possible minute." [7]

The campus outbursts, of course, are as easy to explain as a stampede of Oklahoma cattle, the rutting habits of pronghorn antelope, or the tribal orgies of African aborigines. Apologists suggest that it is merely a case of college boys working off a case of spring fever, letting off steam; psychologists and the yellow journals like to associate the affairs with sex; participants voice no better explanation than the educators. The raids are attributed to anything from an urge to express frustrations and command the attention of an audience to an irrepressible need for venting an excess of good humor.

The good-humor motive may be far fetched for panty raids, but it is as acceptable as any explanation for some of the other gallivanting. It is only fair to credit students with backing up their escapades usually with more humor than perversity; they have a wonderful flair for the absurd and can be the wiliest practical jesters in the entertainment world. An all-too-fastidious dilettante opens his door at 2:00 A.M. after a week end at home to find his room stuffed from wall to wall, floor to ceiling with crumpled newspaper—fifteen hundred cubic feet of wadded pulp—a job that has occupied all the men on a dormitory floor a full afternoon. Or, on the corridor below, a victim who had made the mistake of announcing Friday that he was off on a bender rolls in tipsily on Sunday night, not quite sure of himself, but sure enough to be certain that he is standing on what used to be his south wall. His room has been turned sideways; the pinups and souvenirs are juxtaposed on the floor and ceiling; the rug is centered on the wall with a table precariously resting on it in defiance of the laws of gravity, a chair alongside; the bed, carefully made up, is upended on the same wall.

In technical institutions, where students can rely on their mechanical know-how as well as a greater variety of props from the laboratories, the practical trickery can be even more insidious. A senior at Cal Tech walked into his dormitory room to find a missing automobile completely assembled on his rug, another to encounter a borrowed cement mixer in operation, and a third to buck a giant weather balloon occupying his room—unfortunately filled with water rather than air. Some of the infernally exasperating stunts of the technologists are even good laboratory experiments. A victim was slowly being driven out of his mind by an irritation he couldn't analyze; periodically he squirmed, itched, felt sick to his stomach, couldn't study, couldn't sleep—until he was finally tipped off that a piece of sheet metal activated with a ten-cycle sound frequency, too low for the human ear to pick up, had been hung outside his window.

A distressed freshman appears at the dean's office to confide that he must be cracking up; he can't go to sleep at night because he is forever hearing the sound of dripping water, the ticking of a clock, a rooster crowing, horns honking, the rhythmical surge of ocean, bells of all tones and pitches, the distant roar of a jet, an intermittent snapping as if bones were being broken, accompanied by the faint moan of a dying man. These are old symptoms to the dean; he doesn't send his patient to the psychiatrist. Instead he puts a university electrician on the case and is shortly rewarded with an ingenious homemade loudspeaker which had been lowered into the wall with wires leading to a recorder—and the tormentors.

Much older and more timeworn is the experience of a nervous freshman who sets off a mild explosion with every familiar object he touches; a pop comes out of the keyhole, a crack from the light switch and the knob on the john; the pencil detonates in his hand, as do the buttons on his pajamas, the handle of his toothbrush, the key on his alarm clock. Later he learns that a paste of ammonium tetraiodide when dried is marvelously effective for producing a case of jitters.

Nor is the wit wasted entirely on dormitory mates. A Pomona College coach flung open the door of his apartment one morning in a hurry to get to an appointment. But he didn't use that exit; he climbed out of a window instead. During the night his doorway had been bricked up. Sometimes the jests even take on an international

scope. A fraternity at Ohio State University discovered one morning that its trophy case was empty. Gone was every last hard-earned plaque, cup, and statuette—a collection that had long been useful in persuading eligible freshmen what house they should join. Undoubtedly the trophies had been surreptitiously appropriated by a competing fraternity as a gag, they reasoned; chances of getting them back would be greater if too much of a fuss were avoided. But that confidence was lost with a jolt when a flowery document under the letterhead of a Latin-American bishop arrived at the house one day, thanking the donors profusely for their generous gift and explaining that in accord with their instructions, the *objets d'art* had been melted down, stamped into religious medals, and distributed among the natives.

Deans, of course, have never been able to establish complete immunity from the pranksters. They hurry out from late committee meetings to find that their cars, for some obscure reason, fail to start. They reserve their most kindly manners for innocent dupes who quiver into their offices with forged writs demanding unequivocal explanations for plagiarism on term papers, for acquiring social diseases, or offensive conduct at nonexistent nightspots.

Once in a while the pranks miscarry. The mission assigned by the fraternity pledgemaster to an unwary initiate at an eastern university was to go forth into a frigid winter night and bring back a pussycat obtained by means fair or foul—preferably fair—from some citizen of the city. Knowing that kittens weren't easy to come by on snowy subzero nights, the initiate demurred, so the brothers grudgingly supplied one likely address some distance from the campus. The freshman located the street and number shortly after midnight, rang the bell, and pounded on the door until a baby began squalling upstairs and angry footsteps came thundering down the hall. The door was thrown open and there stood the dean. No, the drowsy receptionist didn't have any spare pussycats, but he did have some strong words of counsel that the petitioner would find it hard to forget.

Still in a temper, the dean was narrating the details of the rough night to his staff the next morning, when an assistant suddenly leaped to his feet. "That explains everything," he exploded. "All night we were hearing strange noises of prowlers in the backyard. My kids are home crying their eyes out because their kitten is gone."

The assistant knew exactly where to find it; he headed for the fraternity house, spurned all denials of complicity from the brothers, and personally began a search of the rooms. He turned up a variety of liquor caches and enough contraband possessions to make them wish they did have a spare cat, but nowhere could the inspector locate so much as a meow. The prosecution of the fraternity for other infringements was well under way when he reached home late that evening to be greeted happily by his children: "We found her in the cellar, Daddy. Pussy wasn't losted at all."

Most annoying to the deans, however, are the anonymous night phone calls. Out of an easy chair the dean pries himself, puts his newspaper down, and answers the ring.

"Is Barney Klugmeyer there?"

"No, Mr. Klugmeyer is not here. You must have the wrong number."

While he is in the shower two hours later again the phone rings. He drips his way to the phone. "Has Barney Klugmeyer come in yet?" asks the same voice.

Again a wrong number.

Then, sometime after midnight, the dean is awakened from broken sleep by still another persistent ring. He stumbles downstairs to hear that familiar voice over the receiver: "This is Barney Klugmeyer. Have there been any calls for me?"

By critics, criminologists, and dissertation-writers the evils of undergraduates have been graded into neat compartments such as mischief, mistakes, malice, mental illness, crime, and delinquency. But actually the efforts prove very little, except to show that the kinds of collegiate misconduct aren't very different from noncollegiate misconduct—if the examples of preposterous "good humor," the less violent outbursts of high spirits, and the practical jests can be left out of consideration. These extras are what confuse the public, raise the most objections, and also raise the question: "What the hell is the younger generation coming to?"

Down the years the younger generations actually haven't changed very much. If anything, campus riots of the mid-twentieth century are more subdued than were the riots of the mid-eighteenth. Contemporary treatment of professors and administration can be very rude, and boisterous, and lacking in feeling for proprieties, but a cannon hasn't been fired at a faculty residence for a great many decades. Buggies and wagons are less frequently found on the roofs of college buildings; cattle are no longer herded into chapels, although a flock of pigeons did recently get loose in a university library. The consumption of goldfish has diminished. In 1899 four hundred pajama-clad University of Wisconsin males marched through the streets of Madison, wedged their way into Ladies Hall and came out with 204 pilfered underthings —a take more profitable per man than the California average.

Intent, as well as appearances, has to be taken into account in judging unconventional deportment of undergraduates. At worst they are trying to badger people, trying to test them with a special kind of all-too-vigorous humor. They want to see how their victim or the audience will react. What they are angling for is a comeback as droll as the challenge they issue—even though it may be a pungent rebuke. They like to tilt for the sport of it, to put the teasing on a give-and-take basis, to parry wit with wit. Frequently the only appropriate response is silence, and even that is respected; they know when a checkmate should be acknowledged, when there is no answer, and are much more interested in getting the acknowledgment than in taking advantage of a victory.

As a protest against a proposed new car restriction under which unauthorized license plates would be deposited in the dean's office, undergraduate opponents went to the trouble of assembling a junk-yard specimen on the portico of the administration building at Oberlin one night. "No plates—but here's the car," read the plaque attached. With a corps of detectives, the culprits could undoubtedly have been run down, but it would have served no purpose. The students merely wanted to register jocular disapproval of the regulations, and it was a good joke—as old as the motor vehicle—but still good to a new generation. The only appropriate thing to do was acknowledge the satire, have the car hauled back to the junk yard, and forget it, and that was exactly what Dean Holdeman did.

All the way up the height of one side of the Hoover tower at Stanford one morning appeared a series of giant footsteps. Some group had gone to an enormous amount of work to place them there and Dean Donald Winbigler suspected who it was. Everybody appreciated the humor. Why kill it? Later, the prints appeared on the other side of the tower, headed down. Then they disappeared. The mystery was never solved, but if Dean Winbigler had decided it was worth spoiling the fun, he could have reached a solution quickly enough, by calling in a few representatives of the Alpine Club.

A lot of disciplining is best left undone—and would be if it weren't for outside pressures. Disciplining deans need to save some of their fire for the more heinous offenses. If students are constantly nagged for off-shade trivialities, they become so inured to admonition that the effect of any reprimand is lost when a serious infraction is denounced. But there is no room for hedging on matters that call for the dean to stand foursquare as the policeman. And here is a range of individual, group, and mass misbehavior that would appear to warrant the establishment of a Scotland Yard on every campus: assault and battery, misappropriation of funds, obscenity in student publications, sexual offenses of every type, theft in all degrees, drunkenness and disorderly conduct, vandalism, forgery, mass disorder, rioting, murder, not to mention the everyday kinds of dishonesty like cheating in examinations and plagiarizing in term papers.

Colleges, of course, get all the blame for harboring the miscreants and tolerating the turbulence. But much of the blaming is misplaced. There isn't a dean in America who hasn't repeatedly had the experience of facing across his desk a parent all too ready to make the confession: "Dean, I've done everything possible to straighten out the boy, and I haven't succeeded. I'm turning him over to you. Do what you can with him." With that unpleasant forewarning, he may conceivably succeed where father and mother have failed, but there are scores of others in the same category on whom there is no advance warning. The police and the paddy wagons pick them up later on.

The student takes to college the moral codes of his family, and the combined undergraduate code will not be much higher than the sum total of the family codes. In order to provide a documented excuse for release from required class work, parents unhesitatingly submit to the dean wonderful fabrications. To get sons out of paying two-dollar fines for parking in areas restricted to visitors, fathers readily swear in writing that they were visiting the college on the date in question and were responsible for the "misunderstanding." In drafting tirades against campus disorders, alumni correspondents overlook the abandon displayed at their own home cocktail parties, the unpublicized affairs at the country club, the revelry

175

at the last business convention. The boys know all about these. A member of that "lost generation" of the '20s, deploring the fix his son was in with a co-ed, called at a dean's office, not to condemn the boy for his libertinism, but to complain about his naïveté, and then freely launched into a discussion of the exemplary manner in which he made his conquests in the 1920s.

Sons brought up in a society where traffic tickets are "fixed," and "swindle sheets" honored, where everyone driving over 65 is taught to keep an eye on the rear-view mirror, where only a sucker pays the list price, where TV, movies, and the pulps advertise the quick advantages in ignoring integrity, can be expected to reflect that society on the campus. If colleges were to adopt the practice of not admitting sons of divorced parents or sons from broken homes, that single measure would eliminate a large percentage of the more serious problems, for it has long been known that this group of students—socially maladjusted, emotionally unstable, cynical, morose—are troublemakers from the start. A dean is doubly conscious of their shortcomings, for his files bulge with the bitter letters from both sides of the family and many of the squabbles are carried on in his office while he sits as intermediary.

Anyone not intimately concerned with college discipline is astonished to learn that many a freshman has never been exposed to the most elementary and vital ethical questions. In counseling a student on the simplest values of honesty, it may be necessary to begin with kindergarten fundamentals. A sophomore accused of turning in a plagiarized paper eventually confessed that he had never in his life submitted an outside English assignment that was his own work. His mother or classmates had prepared most of his high school papers, and college assignments had come from the fraternity "files." The history of a single plagiarized report was traced by one dean so far as it could be traced; the trail led back to an inferior student in a high school five hundred miles from the college; the paper had been freely circulated there. In college the identical paper had been turned in to various instructors no less than a dozen times—graded, incidentally anywhere from A+ to D—.

The distortion of moral values extends to every kind of conduct. When four unmarried couples at an institution in the open spaces of the Far West were apprehended upon their return from an unchaperoned week-end hunting trip, the boys felt that they were entitled to some special dispensation because the girls had proved uncooperative and failed miserably as cooks and camptenders.

"Integrity, like education, is not taught; it is caught," comments a dean of long experience. "All we can do is help students gain an insight into its meaning. We cannot teach it directly, but we can attempt to create an atmosphere of integrity." [8]

Often the operation of the college itself does not offer a very inspiring example of integrity. The higher authorities are too concerned with face-saving and public relations. On the quiet, local police detectives are called in to help identify and round up students suspected of breaking into a college safe. The detectives carry out their

177

job with efficiency, but in the interests of public relations, the college is unwilling to have the criminals prosecuted. In effect the criminals are informed that they are entitled to prolong their adolescence a little longer, in exchange for allowing the college to retain its good name.

"I find that students have a serious question of the integrity of our institutions," interjects Amos Horlacher, former dean at Dickinson College. "For example, sometimes in the way in which we deal with dissenting faculty members, sometimes in the short shrift they get on academic freedom. They wonder whether we are altogether completely honest in the way we get money from business corporations. They have a little concern, I think, as to whether we are always straightforward and fair in explaining things we do . . . Because educational institutions are supposed to have such high purposes, we assume that we do not always have to be straightforwardly honest. The best students that I know on the campuses are really concerned about our integrity." [9]

Piqued when his dean was unable to draw a confession from a student apparently guilty of setting off a barrage of firecrackers in an assembly hall, a president chided his subordinate for not understanding how to handle men. "Send the culprit in to me," he puffed. "I'll settle the matter quickly enough."

The student took his chair opposite the big desk, and the president in his most confidential manner beamed: "Now, son, tell me man-to-man, did you have any part in this unfortunate affair?"

For a long moment the accused deliberated, looking

178

the president squarely in the eye, and finally answered: "Well, Prexy, if you insist on putting it on a man-to-man basis, I'll have to accept the liberty you offer and say that it's none of your damn business."

Deans aren't alone in their failure as disciplinarians.

8.

"JUST A LITTLE BIT AHEAD OF THE STUDENTS"

[*The Dean as Exemplar*]

FOR FIFTY-TWO WEEKS a year, twenty-four hours a day, the dean is on call, constantly plagued with questions that affect the intellectual, moral, and ethical standards of his inquisitors and his college. In his responses he is expected to be uniformly just, reasonable, decisive, and broad-minded—but not too broad-minded. He tries to be the idealist; he has to be the exemplar.

But across the country there is considerable variety in the ideals and examples set: altogether there are some ten thousand American deans, assistants, and administering confederates, as dissimilar as the specialized duties they perform. Along with the warm-hearted humanitarians and efficient professionals is a scattering of ornery executives who bring a great deal of uneasiness to their customers, arbitrary taskmasters prone to accept no back talk, starched scholars contemptuous of anything that falls short of perfection, demanding dictators, pompous bureaucrats, the greeter too damned friendly for comfort, the cautious soul always checking with higher authority, the yes man with an open line to the president's office, the prude with an open line to God.

Deans make mistakes and occasionally apologize for them; sometimes they pull awful bloopers and are sorry, even though they are not at liberty to say so. On the whole, however, there are few classes of public servant with such scrupulous aims and conscientious intentions. If their more reckless critics were to investigate, they would be astonished at the trouble deans take to do the fair thing.

Knowing all too well that they are serving as involuntary exemplars, they do everything that time, patience, and energy allow to put on the right performance. They bone up on how other colleges are handling predicaments like their own; they chew over administrative trends at regional conferences; before making decisions on disciplinary cases, they explore the facts with a dozen faculty and staff members, and, on the side, phone the deans of neighboring colleges for their opinions. A student who spends a tortured night worrying about the plight he is in, and worrying about the inclemency due him, can take a certain amount of malicious comfort in the knowledge that the dean is also having an uncomfortable night.

At one of Boston's more dignified cocktail lounges, a trio of blue-blooded habitués was distracted, baffled, and amused one summer afternoon by a circle of disputatious outlanders who had taken over adjacent tables. The trio didn't make a practice of butting into other people's private affairs, but eavesdropping on this argument was inescapable, for the arguers were virtually making a

181

public hearing out of some minor dishonesty on the part of a fellow named Gordon Eisner, a university law student scheduled to take his bar examinations. Eisner, according to the fragments of evidence, was apparently guilty of having falsified a statement regarding his meal tickets and on the eve of completing his law training, someone had to prepare a character certification for him, with or without reference to the incident of dishonesty. Eisner's future seemed to pivot on the meal tickets and the decision of this group. So what? Who was Gordon Eisner? And who were his censors? Obviously they weren't lawyers, though they seemed to be familiar with the lingo. They didn't have the right cut for government agents, nor the proper hauteur for professors from across the Charles. With the right collars they could have been Episcopal padres; with a little more abandon in their stories, they could have been accepted as sales executives, advertising men, or hotel managers; they seemed to have the fertile look of creative people, and at the same time the bounce of a group of second-string football coaches.

The kibitzers resisted the temptation for a long cocktail hour and at last one of them finally wormed to the edge of the circle, introduced himself to the most accessible member and inquired: "To settle a bet, would you mind telling us your line?"

"Conundrums, sir," was the answer. "We all deal in college conundrums. We are deans of men."

"You mean that it takes twelve deans to settle the predicament of one student?"

"It's much worse than that," answered the respondent.

"We're not all here. There are sixty of us." And then he was back in the fray.

Gordon Eisner was the villain of their current conundrum—the fictitious name of a student at fictitious Ascott University, but the situation a dozen deans were excited about in the cocktail lounge was no fiction. The incident had actually occurred in some college, and, with names and locality suitably disguised, it had become one of the case studies for a seminar at Harvard, where a few dozen deans annually return to school for a week's how-to-do-it refresher. It is only one sample of the effort they make to measure up as exemplars in dispensing justice, fairness, and broad-mindedness.

In the classrooms of the Harvard School of Business Administration, they get down to actualities—analyzing real jams in which deans have become entangled, sticklers that have upset the composure of a whole college family. Everybody pitches in as though the predicament belonged to his own campus. Axes swing to left and right. Chips fly in all directions. No feelings are spared. The student villain may be the one who gets hurt, but it may as likely be the president, a faculty committee or the dean. In the case of Gordon Eisner, Dean Packard's incompetence was as obvious as the law student's indiscretion and, toward the end, the future for Eisner appeared far less bleak than the future for his dean. Summarized one participant after hours of contention, "As Napoleon had his Waterloo, so Dean Packard has earned his Ascott."

In a spirit of good humor and scholarly devotion, they

183

try to puzzle out what move Dean Langston of Merdon State should make next; he has been outspoken in his opposition to Merdon's getting into big-time football; the president, and practically everyone else, is in favor of substantial subsidies for the team, and as the spokesman for the president, Langston is about to take his seat at a meeting of the Board of the Athletic Authority that will make a momentous decision for the future of Merdon. Should Langston come through with one last overwhelming appeal for the liberal education which has made Merdon famous? Should he pocket his own convictions and vote the way the president obviously wants him to? Is there still a chance for compromise? Is his resignation in order?

At conservative Benchley College where an outmoded no-car rule is still on the books, there are several hundred contraband vehicles on the campus; the regulation is warmly supported by parents, by alumni, and by the president (who, incidentally, permits his own student daughter to drive the family car); but Dean Melville and all staff members close to students know that the car rule is unenforceable and unrealistic. The situation is slowly gnawing away at Melville's authority, and, to his embarrassment, the students are convinced he is the principal advocate of the impossible law. How can Dean Melville get off the hook?

Anthony Donato, residence-hall counselor and one-time divinity student at Camoy University, has been so conscientious and sanctimonious about trying to enforce regulations that he has lost control entirely and become the butt of every practical joke in his dormitory. The only students who understand him, he sadly admits, are the doctoral candidates in philosophy. He calls on Dean Driscoll to tell him he is ready to resign and do away with himself. What to do with Donato?

Despite the admonition of the dean, Art Bell, popular editor of *The Daily Blair* at Blair State, continues to publish inflammatory editorials on state politics that are damaging to the University and endangering legislative support. "Liberty of comment is the essence of education," cries Art, sticking to his guns. This brilliant student has been out-foxing the authorities for months and holding the support of his undergraduate clientele in the process. He isn't violating any law and presumably the university should uphold a free press, but the legislators demand that the editor be silenced. Something has to be done about Art. But what? [1]

In their analysis of cases, deans find, ironically enough, that they all too frequently disagree with each other. "On the one hand there are the sharply discriminating and highly intelligent who agree with your point of view," a wrangler points out facetiously, "and on the other, there are those who are rather dull and opinionated and narrow, who disagree." The sessions show the necessity of sorting out facts from opinionated judgments, expose the need for careful, deliberate, objective study from the points of view of all individuals concerned; they provoke self-criticism and self-evaluation, force confident old-timers to review their tactics, demonstrate to dismayed neophytes that there are no ready-made rules for deaning.

Repeatedly the disputants are sidetracked into long

philosophical discussions on how their own backgrounds and personal interests influence diagnosis. They agree that administrators have to stand on principle, but they cannot reach total agreement on the difference between sound principle and deep-seated prejudice. They have to go back and define the fundamental purpose of their administrative effort: not to make people happy, not necessarily to create harmony, but to set the right tone for stimulation of learning and for the development of students morally, intellectually, socially, and physically. There is no way of getting around being the idealist and the exemplar.

In a frank attempt to learn directly from a representative student how well they were measuring up as exemplars, a typical undergraduate president on one occasion was invited to a national conference of deans to tell them exactly what he thought students had a right to expect from a dean. The conferees had a good idea what the answers would be, but they thought it might be a good tonic to hear the response at an occasion where it could be evaluated collectively.

A positive stand was the number-one requisite proposed by their undergraduate accessor. Then, with explanations that indicated he had indulged in some serious reflective homework, he orated on the other attributes: decisiveness, confidence in student leaders, friendship without favoritism, frankness, open-mindedness, a sense of fair play, and empathy—a participation in the student point of view. "We expect you not to forget completely that you were once a student," he added, "that you were once involved with the same temptations, that you once had the same desires. We do not expect you to say *yes* to every program we come up with, but we do expect decisiveness from you whether the decision is on a major problem or a minor one." [2]

The summary checked fairly closely with what the audience expected. For years the thesis had been preached to them by elders in the art of deaning: "The one man who must possess the student point of view is the dean of men—a man who thinks the way his boys think, but who, having a wealth of experience, possessing a reputable character and a wealth of energy, is just a little bit ahead of students; and that little bit, provided he is ahead of the smart ones, is good enough to make a successful dean of men." [3]

Actually the exemplar in the dean's chair has little choice; if he is going to keep ahead of the demands of students, he must always work *with* them, rather than *for* or *against* them, and American undergraduates are the most demanding in the world when it comes to such elements as fair play, justice, open-mindedness, and democratic treatment. Those are accessories paid for with the tuition fee. Students in the United States are as zealously wary of what they like to consider their "institutional prerogatives" as organized labor is of its contract commitments. A miscarriage of justice, withdrawal of some time-honored franchise, a hint of new academic "oppression" brings an immediate retaliatory outburst. Walkouts are uncommon, picketing and violence outmoded, but the same effect is achieved through editorial somersaults, caustic burlesque from the thespians, and very polite acts of organized sabotage.

If there is any possible way of misinterpreting the dogmatisms of the dean, they will find it. "Fraternities have too long been kept on the defensive as a result of public and administrative criticism—much of which is deserved," charged Dean John Hocutt in a fraternity founder's day address at the University of Delaware. Borrowing from football parlance, he pointed out that the best defense is a strong offense. "Fraternity men must take the offensive in introducing constructive programs more in keeping with the lofty purposes set forth in their charters by their founders. They must work unremittingly toward achievements along intellectual, cultural, and charitable lines. When this kind of offensive program becomes the rule rather than the exception," he predicted, "fraternities will meet criticism before it arises and will convert their critics on and off the campus to enthusiastic advocates."

Next day the campus newspaper came from the presses with a banner headline: HOCUTT URGES FRATERNITIES BE MORE OFFENSIVE TO ADMINISTRATION.

In the big universities where the individual can get lost in the crowd, undergraduate vigilance sometimes breaks down, but never in the small college—any institution under three or four thousand. A single student is booted out for unseemly conduct (conduct insufficiently reprehensible according to student standards) and an editor springs to his defense with a diatribe proving that the sole purpose of the dismissal was "to set an example." A fraternity, placed on social probation and deprived of the privilege of scheduling week-end parties, expresses its disapproval by going to the trouble and expense of boarding up every window in the house, festooning it with black crepe, and posting signs: "Quarantined—Social Disease." The administration issues an unheralded edict requiring attendance at one religious service a week, and students dutifully comply with the order, sensing that it is going to be enforced regardless of their sentiments, but they voice poker-faced opposition by overdoing the hymn-singing: drowning out the choir and the organ with unprecedented choral response, gathering on street corners for impromptu renditions of "Holy, Holy, Holy" or "Onward Christian Soldiers," serenading the president's house, the dean's house, and the trustees in session with artful, four-part recitals of "Jesus Wants Me for a Sunbeam," and "Roll, Jordan, Roll."

Because of the sensitivity to interference with "vested privileges and accepted freedoms," it behooves college executives interested in maintaining peace and equanimity on the campus to use exquisite tact in taking official action that affects the undergraduate *status quo.* It is not a question of being timid about getting students riled up; healthy disagreement is essential to any education. Rather it is a question of communication—putting across to students the precise purpose of a decision, justifying it intelligently in terms they will understand. And that is one of the most difficult of all administrative responsibilities.

Actually there is no earthly reason why collegians should feel entitled to such consideration. They attend private colleges on sufferance of the trustees and faculty, and if the catalogue were studied very carefully they would discover that their rights and privileges don't

189

amount to much. But under an educational system groomed for promotion of a free society, they get a great many unspecified benefits—including a voice in the management. This is the American way, and any governing board that tries to buck it will sooner or later be looking for a new president—or a new dean. Even an important research commission of the American Council on Education starts with the basic premise that students, as citizens of a college community, "must participate in its institutional government"; it is the responsibility of every college to develop "a climate in which students have increasing opportunity to serve responsibly and actively in community government."

Students have to be consulted and conditioned before edicts intended to benefit their long-range welfare are issued, and usually the dean is the intermediary. Patient explanations have to be given to groups large and small. Digests of important decisions are sent personally to fraternity presidents and residence-hall managers. The student government president and newspaper editor are briefed on issues at stake. Before a critical letter goes home to parents, it may be reviewed by the student concerned—in the interests of exemplary justice. If a reading knowledge of Russian or a laboratory acquaintance with physics is to be made a new graduation requirement, better to get the students in on the reasoning from the start; if racial discrimination in fraternities is inconsistent with the democratic principles of a university, wisdom dictates that an offending brotherhood be brought in on the argument before laws against discriminatory constitutions are made mandatory; when the estimable Bob Jones steals a volume of the *Encyclopaedia Britannica* from the library, it is well to let the student judiciary help decide whether or not he should be dropped from college.

The eternal vigilance of students in protecting their preconceived notion of veto power keeps the dean-exemplar perpetually on the alert, in constant communication with his fold and his own conscience. And, despite all the precautions, every now and then it will suddenly dawn on him that his trade has fallen off, that his office is suffering a temporary boycott as the result of some breakdown in the communication system. He has no diplomatic immunity. His office is under constant surveillance. His rulings become the *pièce de résistance* at the fraternity dinner table. Any unfairness is detected, discussed, and tucked away for future reference. Not that the students are looking for leniency or blandishment. Even the most stinging penalty is accepted in reasonably good spirit if there is no doubt about its apt application in terms of the crime.

At the expense of censure from the faculty and fellow administrators, occasionally the dean has to take upon himself the sins of his students and, on the strength of his personal faith in their readiness to redeem themselves, crusade in their defense. In fact he may be obliged to take a stand on principle and stake his future on championing the cause of a malefactor whom he has every reason to detest. The only reward he will ever get for his pains comes years later in the form of an embarrassed apology.

While the exemplar is trying to preach democracy, along comes a parent so eager to do the right thing by

191

his boy that he requests a special conference to talk over confidentially the minimum allowance on which a freshman should be able to get along. "I don't want to spoil the boy," says father. "I don't want him to have too much, yet I don't want him to be left out of things because he can't afford to keep pace. We're ready to make a sacrifice. If we pay the tuition and other college charges, do you think he could get along on five hundred a month?"

Or another parent—father of a star halfback—who purchases a $40,000 house in the college town to be used for entertaining his friends on week ends when they fly in for the games. Or the overprotective mother who shepherds her son through the maze of registration desks and knows all the answers until she approaches the counter where student cars are supposed to be registered. Stymied there, she calls the clerk to ask for dispensation. "We really can't register the car today," she apologizes, "we haven't decided whether Archibald should have the Lincoln or one of the Cadillacs."

After delivering a bright message on the virtues of assuming personal responsibilities to a block of 5000 undergraduates, a dean receives an emergency phone call from a distracted mother who wants to know where her son is. He was due home fifteen minutes ago. It is shocking to her that the university can't keep closer track of the boys.

And while he is preaching integrity, the university itself announces with appropriate fanfare and respect the acceptance of a magnanimous gift from a tycoon who is liberally flayed in the economics texts for his cunning financial manipulations.

Meantime, playful academic hecklers are chiding the

dean for trying to make things easy for himself by molding a student body of conformists, to the detriment of the creative spirit, the exploring mind, and the will to experiment. It is true that he demands conformity, but only in the sense that rigid discipline is essential to any professional training: whether it is nuclear physics or music, law, medicine, or poetry. It is reasonable to insist that social conformity be an integral part of the professional discipline.

"We must accomplish something more than keeping the peace, assuaging the public opinion about our institutions, or deluding our superiors into thinking that they preside over passive and stereotyped student citizens," asserted one dean. "Ours is perhaps the greatest opportunity in the whole academic community to teach practically through real social situations the meaning of freedom, and the obligations of free men and women." [4]

Teaching these social obligations—lessons of charity for minority groups, partnership in community enterprise, extension of democracy to the less privileged—is perhaps the most knotty assignment the dean has, and usually it is necessary to go at it the hard way by dropping random suggestions, setting examples that will eventually come back in the form of student inspirations after their origin is forgotten. Once students hitch their wagons to a star of their own discovery, amazing things happen. Movements sweep across the country, exhibitions of idealism that are most difficult to associate with panty-raiding, fish-swallowing, car-smashing youngsters.

At Bowdoin in 1947 a junior named Joe Wheeler took on a brotherhood-of-man obsession. If every fraternity in the United States, he reasoned, had but one student from a foreign country as a houseguest, exchanging ideas, swapping viewpoints at bull sessions and table arguings, adding a new dimension to their living, the total contribution toward international understanding would be incalculable. Hesitantly he took the scheme to Dean Nathaniel Kendrick, who had long been trying to spark this kind of idealism without being too obvious about it.

Within months Joe's dream was a reality. All twelve chapter houses at Brunswick unanimously voted to go in on it. The fraternities would furnish free lodging, meals, and incidentals; the college would take care of tuition; the Institute of International Education would cooperate.

From the start, the experiment was a glowing success, and was soon being adopted by fraternities in scores of other colleges. Within ten years Bowdoin students had acquired firsthand an entirely new conception of international relations from representatives of twenty-five different countries, and Bowdoin and the United States had some very warm friends in far-off places like Vietnam and the Ryukyu Islands, Venezuela and Costa Rica, Hungary and Czechoslovakia. One foreign guest spoke for them all: "In the unique atmosphere of a small and old liberal arts college in America, in the comradeship and friendship of a fraternity, in the kind of education system which has its aim equally in imparting knowledge and the development of the individual, a whole new world opened itself to me—the world of American literature and history, of what seemed to me a freer way of thinking, a world and a country of which I had heard many true and many false things previously and yet knew nothing about." That single response can be multiplied by thousands from other colleges across the nation.

The reception of foreign students beyond the campus limits, however, isn't always as cordial as it is in the fraternity house. They are in demand as speakers and panel participants at women's organizations, schools, and Rotary Clubs, but they also encounter antagonists who think that American higher education should be reserved for Americans. The foreign-student program at a university in Kansas, which included some thirty representatives from the Middle East, was all but disrupted by the prejudice of a single sheriff. He wanted to run every last Moslem and Hindu out of the county. To be sure, the visitors did give the sheriff a hard time. In trying to conform to American mores, their first act was to purchase a car; their second to ram something with it. Whether they came from Pakistan, Iraq, or Egypt, to the vigilante they were all "camel drivers," and the dean had to make a daily run between his office and the county seat in response to the sheriff's exultant phone messages: "Hey, dean, I got another one of your camel drivers here in jail."

The alertness with which foreign students catch on to American mores—or their conception of them—is apt to bring mortification to both the foreigners and their hosts. At a West Coast university every front window of a fraternity house was shattered one night and the chaplain, living across the street, thrown out of bed, when some prankster blew up the statuesque Sigma Alpha Epsilon lion with a super-charge of dynamite. The insurrectionist never was identified, but a foreign student, sensing the

195

tragic loss to the Sigma Alphas and having observed the freedom of conscience with which his fellow collegians appropriated private property, took it upon himself to hire a van and pick up a substitute lion, four feet long and weighing half a ton, that guarded the gate of a nearby country estate. Lacking some of the sleight-of-hand subtlety of his associates, the foreigner had hardly finished his speech of presentation when he was pounced upon by a bevy of policemen, by the indignant owners of the masonry, by innocent Sigma Alphas—with the dean and a bruised chaplain trying to intercede for him.

And at an East Coast university a new arrival from Nigeria, who took to all the other campus customs almost too avidly, still couldn't stoop to wearing Western attire. It made him feel too conspicuous, he explained. Donning his usual cotton pajamas, a skull cap, and a loose-flowing robe of gaudy stripes, he set out alone to explore the town after getting his institutional bearings. Spectators were relatively polite in their staring, and all went well with him until he reached a downtown restaurant. There the Nigerian in his billowing finery spotted his first two American gangsters. He recognized them instantly from the movies he had attended back in Africa. Their hats had the authentic slouch, their cigarettes hung at the right angle, their talk came from one corner of the mouth. He sidled up to them to catch snatches of their conversation, and to his horror learned that they were on the trail of a waitress at the lunch counter inside. They were plotting to get her for Friday night. Recalling the role of Hollywood hero, the Nigerian at once realized that it was his responsibility to protect the heroine. As covertly as

the robes allowed, he slipped through the door, took a stool at the counter, and ordered a cup of coffee. But unfortunately one of the gangsters was close behind him and took an adjacent seat before he could issue his warning to the waitress.

As the gangster chatted amiably, making obvious progress with his prey, the Nigerian attempted to convey to her some hint of her peril by shaking his head, rolling his eyes, waving his fingers. She didn't seem to respond to his signals. In desperation he drafted an admonition on a scrap of paper and slipped it to her from under his sleeve when next she passed. Even that she seemed to misinterpret. He suddenly realized that, instead of reacting to his overtures, she was phoning the police to report his actions. This wasn't at all in accord with the Hollywood script. Utterly baffled, he dodged out of the restaurant and took a taxi back to the university. It was the dean, of course, who had to pacify the police and explain to the Nigerian that the gangsters were harmless agents of the Federal Bureau of Investigation.

With a great deal of behind-scenes prompting from deans, fraternities have been mending local as well as international fences since World War II. Usually it has started with the substitution of "Help Week" for "Hell Week"—that legacy of an older, heartier generation that went in for bruised bottoms, branding irons, forty-mile hikes, and unfraternal humiliation during initiation rites. The days of paddling are not entirely done for, but some of the energy that formerly went into the memorable horseplay has been transferred into charitable, constructive endeavor, and during initiation week fraternity work parties take time out to do a paint job on a run-down country church, to repair the roof over the head of an impoverished octogenarian, reorganize the books in the town library, or convert a neglected park into a pleasant picnic area. Sometimes the motive behind all the labor is a little shallow, merely a conspicuous attempt to make amends for too-well-publicized past dereliction, but for the most part the jobs are done with astonishing enthusiasm and finesse; in fact, a fraternity may become so engrossed in its effort that a moldering institution is "adopted," infused with new zest, and brought back to life.

In their spare time and with a minimum of effort, college students can readily maintain their reputation for being as undomesticated as a pack of metropolitan delinquents, but, when they put themselves to it, they can almost as easily be charming bearers of good will to a local populace. Stanford University fraternal and other student groups virtually run a convalescent home for crippled children on the edge of the Palo Alto campus. They volunteer spare-time services, contribute thousands of dollars a year for medical aid and operational expenses, and cunningly associate it with their undergraduate judicial system by assigning offenders to work there. When pranksters were nabbed for dropping water bombs from the rafters of a theater during the flicks, each was sentenced to twenty hours of charitable labor at the home. Even the University of California judicial council in a spirit of cooperation and good humor on one occasion committed three of their undergraduates, found guilty

199

of painting up the Stanford campus, to work at the convalescent home.

Christmas parties for underprivileged town kids have become a tradition in hundreds of fraternities and, if anything, the boys get a bigger kick out of the entertainment than their guests. On one night a year just before the holidays, the house is turned into a toyland overrun with a screaming mob of infants. The hosts think of everything: a big tree, festive decorations, stockings stuffed with candy, a convincing Santa Claus, cookies, goodies, music, games, and a shower of presents that would make any child's eyes glow. They cheerfully mop up the puddles, join in the floor games, and get a little choked up when a six-year-old ragamuffin can't comprehend that the heavy blue sweater and the magnificent doll thrust into her arms are both hers.

At Williamstown, Massachusetts, town and gown joined forces in 1953 to produce a bicentennial celebration that would be remembered until the tricentennial was due. Dean Robert Brooks was the chief entrepreneur, taking a lead in the big stage production, editing a new historical volume, and helping with plans for a spectacular parade. But the biggest challenge he and his cohorts took on was constructing a replica of the first pioneer cabin built in the region. For it they agreed to handicap themselves by using only the tools and materials available in 1753. Timbers for the oak frame were hand hewn and lugged out of the woods by volunteers, clapboards and shakes were rived by hand from billets of ash, the interior was plastered with a mixture of clay and straw. For every hour of labor that went into the project, accurate accounts were kept, and when the final tally was made, exemplar Brooks had put in exactly 1108 hours.

Inevitably the dean's office becomes a relief center when disaster strikes a region that has a college within phoning distance. From that office, squads of students go forth to fight fires and salvage property. They're johnnies-on-the-spot when it comes to hurricane relief in the east, clearing up after tornadoes in the midwest, rescuing from fire and flood in the west. At 1:30 one morning Dean Hopkins at the University of Massachusetts received a phone call from the chief of police in a neighboring village, reporting that a three-year-old girl was missing from her home. Could the dean round up a dozen men or so to join a search party?

Within an hour close to five hundred students were piling into ninety cars. "That search party," says Dean Hopkins, "rolled out of the main parking area in a manner which could have made any commanding officer of a military unit proud; there was no hesitation, there was no boisterousness, there was ample distance between cars, there was no pushing and shoving." They combed the designated area for two hours and shortly before daybreak one of the men caught a glimpse of a suspicious bundle huddled in some leaves. He picked up the lost three-year-old, nearly frozen, hungry and terrified. And, according to the report that came back, the rescuer just stood there with the child in his arms, tears rolling down his cheeks.

This kind of compassion, however, doesn't come undiluted, and the dean is very much aware that youthful excesses can easily turn from one direction to another.

201

The heartwarming Christmas party for the kids may be followed by a beer bust that leaves the fraternity house a shambles. Charity toward Hungarian nationals is balanced by ostracism of a native Jew. One fraternity is courageously laying plans for a break with its national in order to pledge a Negro, while another is deciding to disband rather than comply with the integration policies of the institution. The process of trying to evoke consistent idealism in students is not merely frustrating; sometimes it appears all but futile.

Just before vacations, when undergraduate resistance to precept attains a peak and the patience of deans a nadir, the situation is roughest. In one of the off-guard communiqués that one dean sends to another in search of sympathy, a dejected representative exploded on December 14: "On a day like this a dean counts his blessings and the tail-lights of twelve hundred cars—cars bearing four thousand students away from town. It isn't that we don't love each and every one of them, but we are delighted that they are to continue their Christmas merriment somewhere else. Last night they gave parties for the little grade school children—the prettiest exhibition of Christian good will you'd find anywhere. They outdid themselves—and then outdid themselves again in exhausting any entitlement to reprieve they felt they had earned. The kegs and the bottles came out of hiding and in the free-for-all that went on into the small hours, they laid the dining hall in ruins, stole the bulbs out of the tree in the town park, ripped the telephones out of most of the dormitories. Now as suave intellectual young men, they are ready to go home to their proud papas and mamas. The Christmas spirit is abroad—not here. They took it with them."

Job is the only mortal who would have made the perfect dean.

9.

"VERY PRESENT HELP IN TROUBLE"

[The Dean as Benefactor]

FIGURE ON $600 from the folks, summer earnings of $450, $400 from campus employment, and a loan or scholarship of $300. Total $1750—about what a year in college averages. Costs at a state university may run two or three hundred less; at a private college or technical institute at least that much more. And the sources can be juggled to suit one's purse, pride, and enterprise.

Since World War II a few teen-age tycoons have actually paid all their college expenses and made money on the side. A University of North Carolina undergraduate set himself up as a book salesman and not only wrote his own checks for all university charges, but also purchased a car for himself and a piano for his less affluent mother. A Cornell huckster who took on a concession for selling vegetable-slicing machines promoted so much business that he had to hire eighteen fellow students as assistant salesmen. A Washington University pre-med aspirant, realizing that he had a long haul ahead, spent a few months qualifying as a first-class carpenter before matriculating, hammered his way through the under-graduate years in St. Louis (at $2.50 an hour), then went on to medical school, supporting a wife and three children at the same time. And an Ivy Leaguer at Yale espoused the pants-pressing business and made enough money in four years to consider retirement, but instead of retiring, he stayed in business and became a multimillion-aire before he was thirty.

However, it isn't as easy as it sounds. Of the three and a half million undergraduates in the United States, 3,499,999 seem to have a rough time making ends meet, and despite the millions in college scholarship aid, the subsidies from the foundations, and the well-publicized generosity of big industry, stretching educational dollars becomes increasingly difficult as the enrollment of three and a half million gradually multiplies itself toward the six million anticipated by 1970.

The popular misconception that private colleges have suddenly turned moneygrubbing grows from the fact that for three centuries they were anonymously paying the lion's share of instructional costs out of income from invested endowment funds; they can no longer afford it. The gratuity system worked marvelously while a student body remained in the hundreds, but when enrollment doubled, tripled, and quadrupled into the thousands without a corresponding increase in endowment returns, the cut for any one individual diminished enigmatically. At the same time frugal standards in undergraduate living were exchanged for country-club standards, instructional costs mounted, educational equipment and special-

205

ized curricula became infinitely more expensive. Someone had to pay for the refinements as well as take up the slack, and quite logically the bill went to the immediate beneficiary.

Alumni who thought that fifty or a hundred dollars a semester was a stiff tuition tax back in the 1920s now wince at assessments of $450 or $500 for their sons. And even then few of them realize that nearly a third of the actual cost is a hidden gratuity. If the pinch could only have been foreseen, college management would long ago have impressed students with the kind of philanthropic dole they were drawing, and started preparing them by easy stages for the inevitable change. Fees were increased steadily between 1940 and 1952, but not nearly enough to correspond with rising living costs. A hike of 100 per cent during that period would have permitted a much easier transition.

The current generation of students has adjusted itself to the new economic order in higher education far more readily than its parents. For the less privileged, undergraduates seeking summer employment and odd jobs between classes is an American convention as old as Harvard, but now the opulent have joined the insolvent, and a record of vacation experience carries more weight with industrial recruiters than club memberships and athletic distinctions. Pride be hanged, boys with Westchester County addresses fight fires in the Northwest, dig clams on the Maine coast, or operate oil rigs in Texas.

The 1958 recession at least temporarily affected the market for undergraduate labor, eliminating many of the "good deals" and restoring popularity to camp counseling and hotel jobs at which students had been lifting their noses for a decade or two. But even in hard times, an energetic and lucky job-seeker can hope to clear expenses and make a minimum of three or four hundred dollars during a summer. An up-early, to-bed-late Amherst sophomore held down two jobs; he drove a milk wagon mornings, worked with a construction gang afternoons, and by September had a bank balance of $2900.

Distance from home lends a strange kind of educational enchantment. Students from the Far West like to head east, the eastern lads head west. A freshman hitchhiker set out from Hanover, New Hampshire, carrying an overnight kit and a big sign advertising a Dartmouth-to-New Mexico itinerary, and three days later notified his anxious parents from Santa Fe that he was profitably set up on a dude ranch; the whole trip had cost him exactly $1.87—mostly for hamburgers and busfares through cities. But Dartmouth erudition clashed with New Mexican preferences on the ranch, so he moved on to a Colorado resort and by September wound up as assistant to a hotel manager with $750 in his pocket. First question popped to him when he arrived back in New Hampshire was how much of that $750 he had squandered on his return trip. "Oh, I took it easy coming back," he maintained. "It cost much more than going out. Besides I had to pay twenty-five cents for walking across a toll bridge." His travel expenses were $2.44 on the trip back.

Starting the summer as a messenger at a New York air terminal, a sophomore from Vermont began making suggestions for speeding up traffic on nonscheduled airlanes. On the strength of his show of initiative, he was promoted to clerk, but he was too good for that job, too. As traffic expediter he spent most of July, August, and September flying from coast to coast or north and south untangling knots in flight service and drawing a princely salary. Two days before college was due to open, he turned up on his campus to expedite the settlement of some academic deficiencies carried over from the previous year, but he was unable to comply with proposals made by the dean because he was obliged during those two remaining days to make one more ten-thousand-mile hop to Mexico City by way of Los Angeles. He was back in time for his first class, with enough capital to get married and see himself through graduation.

Students show amazing finesse in lining up jobs on their own, angling for scholarships and loans, or hatching good reasons why the old man or Uncle Oscar should come through with another five hundred. But in one capacity or another the dean is usually called in on the deal. He is a sort of agent in undergraduate philanthropy; he runs an employment office for part-time or summer work, has a hand on the purse strings of the revolving loan fund, is the ever-ready reference, and has a controlling interest in the scholarship assets. He is the broker who takes calculated risks in investing college resources where the highest dividends will be paid in student achievement, and he has to be pretty cold-blooded about it sometimes, for though the scholarship budget may be in six big figures, the sum is never big enough. One of his more irksome errands is warding off the mob who are sure that cut rates for education are as common as cut rates for automobiles and household appliances.

Orthodox scholarship awards are based on above-average grades, financial need, and good character—past performance and future promise—but the broker has to be on the lookout for both the "late bloomer" and the "early fader"—the man who has never had an opportunity to demonstrate his real capabilities, and the man who has already dazzled his following with prep-school achievements and will try to coast through college on old honors. Then he has to be equally wary of parsimonious parents who are convinced that the world and the college owe their gifted son a free ride and will indulge in anything short of fraud to prove it.

To contend with the sharpers as well as to provide a fairer deal for the overscrupulous, trickproof questionnaires as complicated as income-tax forms have been worked out by a national organization known as the College Scholarship Service. The purpose of the Service is to eliminate some of the competitive intercollegiate bidding for the superior candidates and to conserve funds for use where they are most needed by encouraging colleges to accept common standards for measurement of financial needs and by promoting research on the effectiveness and failings of scholarship programs. John U. Monro, Director of the Financial Aid Office at Harvard, is the father of this service, and in less than a decade he has done more to advance the cause of equitable distribution of scholarship funds than other educators have in a century. "There is no doubt that we are in a period of very rapid change and development in the financial aid business," he claims. The problem is getting so big that it is ceasing to be the assignment, part-time, of an otherwise busy-enough dean; and there is emerging on the scene a new college officer known as the financial aid officer. Colleges are going through the process of bringing together the scholarships, loans, and jobs under one administrative control. We are learning to use loans. We are learning how to measure need, and how not to give scholarships to able and attractive young people if they have no need. Colleges are as responsible as anyone else for the fact that a large proportion of our brightest young people never get an advanced education. We are recruiting competitively, all concentrating on a few extremely able students, and the impression has got around that only the brightest can get help. The one big accomplishment yet to come will be the coordination of effort in recruiting able admission candidates of impoverished backgrounds and persuading them that they can go to college.

"American colleges are about fifty years behind the times in developing a liberal and business-like system of long-term credit for students and parents," Monro continues. "At a time when the American customer has learned to buy all manner of capital goods on easy time payments, colleges for the most part have hung back, regarding loans as a relatively unpopular form of aid, a burden to the student, something of an administrative nuisance to administer. The general preference for scholarships is easy to understand but it is an expensive taste, and will surely break down at the next turn of the inflationary wringer."

Most deans are not over-optimistic about ever being entirely relieved of the headaches brought on by lack of funds for deserving students, but very generally they do recognize that one of the best remedies will be found in college loans—which are usually interest-free until after graduation and then carry a rate of only three or four per cent, with broad latitude for repayment. However, convincing their clientele of that conviction is a slow process. Almost half the colleges in the United States have substantial loan funds that have been going begging for years. Students just didn't want to go into debt. With all the talk about fat, full-expense athletic scholarships, industrial handouts, and other bounties, the impression was circulated that only a dope would stoop to borrowing, though actually when all the free awards were totaled and divided by the number of recipients, the average scholarship was less than $250, and only one in five students got any lift at all. The men ready and willing to borrow money for long-range educational financing have been those who prove to be the most eligible candidates for scholarships. But it is a certainty that the loan is at last beginning to find a proper place in the budget.

Since the installment plan has invaded every other phase of economy, administrators are convinced that it should be applied also to payment of tuition bills. A few colleges have already adopted alternative schemes which allow for monthly rather than semester payments; private finance organizations have similar arrangements, and insurance companies provide for a spread of charges over a period of twenty years or longer.

Princeton's treasurer has advanced the radical idea that all tuition charges be doubled and that higher education be put on a Study-Now-Pay-Later basis. According to his scheme, students would merely sign IOUs for their tuition; these notes would be sold at a small discount to a "General Educational Acceptance Corporation," which would in turn do the collecting and spare treasurers the disagreeable task of hounding graduates for their monthly payments. Special provision for students entering poorly paid but socially useful professions would be made in the form of "retroactive scholarships" which would cancel all or part of the debt obligation.

The plan raises some ticklish questions, however, suggests a financial editor: "For one thing colleges would have to decide whether retroactive scholarships should be limited to teachers, ministers, social workers, and the like, or whether they would also be granted to poets, painters and housewives. The housewife presents a particularly awkward dilemma, since the scheme might result in pricing some college women out of the marriage market. A young Princeton A.B., for instance, might well hesitate to marry a Vassar girl who owes the General Acceptance Corporation $28.35 a month for ten years." [1]

Regardless of whether a Study-Now-Pay-Later plan or some other installment scheme comes into vogue, hard-pressed undergraduates of the future who cannot foot the ever-mounting tuition and service charges will be obliged to break down and borrow. There simply aren't enough free grants to go around. In the Ivy League a scholarship is available for every fourth student, but that average will not hold up in many other institutions. Moreover, the boys who make small undergraduate fortunes as air-traffic expediters, carpenters, and pants pressers, despite the publicity they acquire, are an even smaller minority than the big scholarship holders. Seven out of every ten students encounter serious financial troubles of one sort or another, estimates one authority—and where there is trouble for the students, there is also trouble for the dean.

With frugal habits and a great deal of self-denial, it was possible in the 1920s to work one's way through college, and it is still done, though every dean in the country will explain that it is next to impossible unless a student brings to college a trade or a rare talent. Very few are interested even in attempting the ordeal, and the attitude of parents has changed too; where fathers once insisted that sons earn their way, they are now more likely to insist on paying it—to avoid the hardships they suffered. In addition, a strong phalanx of students is brought up to be contemptuous of manual labor, or any labor short of the executive variety.

At colleges located near large metropolitan centers there are always more part-time jobs than there are takers, though over three quarters of the students at a university like UCLA earn some of their expenses. Admissions officers at Harvard, the University of Chicago, and Stanford assure any prospective freshman that they will find him all the spare-hour work he wants. At Ohio State over 80 per cent of all financial aid is in the form of jobs, and several thousand earn an average of $600. Yale is so hepped on teaching the lessons of Yankee self-reliance that assistance is offered in a package—a work-loan-scholarship combination. Then a number of small colleges and technical schools run co-op plans under which students work part of each year in an industrial

213

plant and take five or six years to get a degree.

Impressive, indeed, is the compensation at well-situated institutions. The physical science laboratory at New Mexico A and M alone has a student payroll of a quarter of a million dollars annually—larger than the total instructional payroll. Located near the rocket and guided missile center at White Sands Proving Grounds, the laboratory has government contracts which call for a vast amount of data reduction and basic or applied research, and although a single student is limited to twenty hours per week, many a budding physicist earns as much as $1000 a year between classes.

From the students' point of view, the one irreconcilable flaw in the undergraduate aid program is the athletic scholarship. To them it is both inconsistent and unprincipled. For two decades they smiled knowingly at the special favors extended to the boys of brawn and cheered them on, but under more straitened circumstances they are no longer smiling or cheering. Free tuition, free board, room, books, and brain feeding for the athletes is an anachronism, they reason; if the university can afford to play Santa Claus to the muscle men, there ought to be more stuffing for the stockings of those with intellectual prowess. This debunking of athletic commercialism may be a passing, artificial undergraduate fashion that will last only until the football team starts losing games regularly, but the rah-rah spirit is now perpetuated principally by the alumni, while the younger generation nurses its resentment. The ball-carriers are applauded on Saturday afternoons, but students are inclined to ignore or ridicule them the rest of the week; the dormitory that is used to house grid heroes is referred to unkindly as "the Zoo" and the dining hall where they are fed their red-meat diet as "the Ape House."

Most deans are as much aware of the hypocrisy in subsidies for athletes as are the students, but they have long since lost authority in the matter. The athletic colossus is one of the income-producing fixtures of the great university, and a recognized advertising medium; any alteration in its superstructure is a question of the gravest import to be decided by the trustees, the regents, or the state legislature. Deans are constantly reminded of the perversion, for the administration of any honest program of student aid has to be based consistently on genuine need, creditable character, and intellectual resourcefulness, without partiality for unscholarly attributes.

However, athletic ability is not the only bias that has to be considered in awarding scholarships. Every institution has on its books an odd assortment of honoraria which must be parceled out under the terms of the original bequest to a preferred few. There are special scholarships which may be allotted only to Murphys, Andersons, or Pennoyers; scholarships for sons of ministers, missionaries, and musicians; a great many awards established by inveterate golfers of the 1920s for personable caddies; at one university a substantial grant (usually unclaimed) awaiting a male harpist; a very old bequest for the benefit of a lad who never has and never will use tobacco or snuff in any of its insidious forms; scholarships for Boston newsboys, sons of San Francisco cab drivers, sons who can boast at least one parent born in Sweden, in Italy, in China, or some other country; and a vast number of obscure catalogue listings for boys born in particular towns and counties. The critics can easily argue that if special scholarships may be awarded to harpists, to golf caddies, and Pennoyers, why should a dean object to making similar grants to halfbacks and shortstops?

"Many colleges with large scholarship programs have never defined for themselves exactly what they are trying to do with their funds, chides John F. Morse, Vice-president at Rensselaer Polytechnic Institute. Attempting to sift fact and popular hearsay, he adds, "It is safe to say that applicants who show through such standard measuring devices as the Scholastic Aptitude Test that they possess outstanding ability have a better chance of winning aid than have those of average ability. It is a fact that most colleges, rightly or wrongly, prize what is called the 'all-round' man, and that a standard measurement for this all-roundness is participation in extracurricular activities. So these activities assume vast importance for the scholarship applicant. It is a fact that almost every college, rightly or wrongly, prizes geographical distribution and is willing to pay round-trip fares to get it. It is, therefore, in general easier for a student to get a scholarship in a college 1,000 miles from home than it is to get one in his own state. It is a fact that many colleges prize athletic distinction and that they have, therefore, devoted increasingly large amounts of money to subsidizing students who do not necessarily possess any of the other talents the colleges prize, but do possess extraordinary physical talents. It is a fact that colleges devote their scholarship funds in direct proportion to those talents they most highly prize, and that in general they use those funds to strengthen those parts of their programs they feel to be weakest. And, finally, it is a fact that most colleges devote their scholarships to those who need them, and it is my opinion that this last makes all the abuses and misuses relatively unimportant." [2]

In addition to the assorted college antes, hundreds of attractive premiums have been set up during the past decade by business corporations, ranging from Pepsi-Cola and Shell Oil to Eastman Kodak and Westinghouse; these were topped by the National Merit Scholarships; and then came the prospect of generous federal scholarship aid. But if all the available amounts were evenly distributed among three and a half million collegians, each would get just about enough to cover the overhead for a good party week end.

To the dean, every student in need of aid is an individual problem. He may be helped most readily by an outright grant, if it is available, by part-time work, by a loan, by living in a cooperative house where he can cut down on his room and board bill while washing dishes, sweeping corridors, or cooking spaghetti. It may be a combination of any or all of them. Occasionally, after considering the assets and liabilities, the dean forthrightly recommends that a student pull out of college and work for a year or two until he can return with the necessary resources; and just as often all the down-and-outer needs is a little encouragement, a pat on the back, and a five-dollar bill.

"Only once during the four years did the outlook seem entirely hopeless," wrote an alumnus who had worked his way through Harvard during Dean Briggs' regime. "That was in the spring of my senior year. . . . One morning as I went to classes, I spent my last cent on car fare. I wore two rubbers for the left foot, and the world looked gloomy indeed. To make matters worse, the mail man passed me a note from the dean asking me to call at his office at noon, and I wondered what new troubles were about to descend.

"At the dreaded hour I knocked at his door. He stepped into the hall and in a stammering way said: 'I hardly know how to begin. Some years ago a man in the Law School died, and for several years his sister used to send me five dollars to give to some student who could not go home for Christmas. Recently one of the men to whom I gave the five dollars returned and gave me back the five dollars doubled. Now I wonder if you would feel hurt if I should ask you to accept the ten dollars which he just gave me?' To my dying day I shall always wonder how Dean Briggs knew of my financial condition." [3]

It is a startling revelation to undergraduate critics to learn that the traditional snooping dean has other purposes than uncovering scapegraces. By the same mysterious means that Dean Briggs used in 1898 to discover his penniless student, a dean in a southwestern college in 1958 turned up a married couple living in a trailer "so poor that they ate no breakfast, day after day had one cheese sandwich apiece for lunch, and cornflakes and milk for dinner." The husband was a brilliant physics major, but failing because he was so hungry all the time he could not study effectively, and the wife couldn't hold a job for the same reason. When their situation was sized up, college was clearly beyond their means, and the only logical advice the dean could give them was to quit until they had a few hundred dollars in the bank. But he withheld that advice for a time, found a temporary job for the wife, and some pocket money for her husband. Then, when their stomachs were full and their spirits fortified, they were gently persuaded to check out. He helped make arrangements for the student to return to an excellent job with a gas company, saw that he was enrolled in a night physics class at a junior college and his wife enrolled in a secretarial course. They happily left the trailer camp, knowing that they would be welcomed back the following year with a scholarship waiting for him and a better secretarial position for her.

The greatest satisfaction a dean can get comes from identifying his campus waifs and giving them a lift. That kind of gratification was felt by Dean William Craig when he found Beryl Blue Spruce on the Stanford campus. Beryl was an Indian from New Mexico, self-reliant, intelligent, and unswerving in his ambition to return to his Navajo village eventually as an M.D. and be of service to the people whom he loved and who needed him. But he was terribly handicapped by inadequate college preparation and inadequate funds, and handicapped further by the old tribal tradition which decreed that an Indian of twenty-five should be supporting his parents. He needed to spend every waking hour with his books, but in order to make ends meet and send an occasional token dollar to his father, he felt obliged to take on any odd job he could find—table waiter, gardener, gas-pump operator, garage mechanic's helper, and, during the summers, attendant at a mental hospital in New Mexico. He was almost ready to give up when Dean Craig learned of his plight, assigned him a scholarship, found him work that would bring in regular income, and started him on a plan that would enable him to realize his ambition.

In a chilly rooming house on another campus, a dean came across a Hungarian student, holed up by himself during Christmas vacation, depressed, woefully lonely, suffering from hypertension, and dieting on canned baked beans. Nicholas relished a beef roast at the dean's table that night, and it was over coffee that he told the kind of story that has become familiar in many a college town: a secure life in Budapest suddenly shattered by the coming of the Communists, his father shot before his eyes, his mother unable to support the big family. To relieve the demands on his mother, he wandered away from home when still a child, working when he could find work, attending school whenever and wherever he could, barely keeping alive. Rather than any physical sustenance, faith and hope of freedom kept him going. Eventually he did make a dramatic escape to Austria, and after weeks of interrogation was allowed to enroll in an Austrian university. There an announcement of United States scholarships was brought to his attention. He applied, was accepted, and at the age of 26 entered an American college—still too proud to admit the desperation of his circumstances.

Within a few days of his discovery, Nicholas was living in a free room at a fraternity house, had a job in the college dining hall, and money for incidentals from the undergraduate council in addition to his full-tuition scholarship. His adopted country needs science teachers, he has learned, and he hopes to repay his debt by teaching young Americans, but on the side he also intends to find a way to help his countrymen out of their insufferable dilemma.

Rather than face the maze of red tape in the treasurer's office or call on some charitable organization, the dean is forever reaching into his own pocket to help somebody— five dollars for an emergency trip home, ten bucks to bribe a salvageable apostate to attend a conference on religion at another college, a loan of fifteen to ease the ire of a landlady and save a man from eviction. He robs the home wardrobe of a windbreaker for a foreign student shivering in his one threadbare sack coat. On faith, hope, and charity, he endorses notes that the comptroller's office refuses to honor. He furnishes bail for jugged lawbreakers, and every few days teases his wife with a phone call to report that he is bringing the hungry Hans Wolfinger or the depressed Tommy Nishimura home for dinner.

After addressing an out-of-town parent-teacher group, Dean Baldwin of Cornell was approached by an enthusiastic mother who eagerly announced that she had a sterling son at Cornell of whom she was very proud. Surely the dean, with some 8000 students, wouldn't know him! Dean Baldwin guessed that she was probably right, but he politely inquired the boy's first name.

Charlie Walters? Oh, yes, the dean knew him very well, and as evidence, he efficiently reeled off exact information on how Charlie was doing in each of his classes, reported guardedly on his deportment, his health, his social adjustment at Ithaca, and his extracurricular interests.

Mrs. Walters fluttered off to find her husband so that

he too could meet the wonderful dean who kept in such close touch with his students. Under the circumstances, Dean Baldwin considered it inappropriate to explain why he happened to be so familiar with the record of this pillar of virtue—whom he had seen several times during the past twenty-four hours. Burning in his pocket was a ten-dollar bill which Charlie had returned to him that very morning as reimbursement for bail the dean had paid to release him from the city jail where he had spent the previous night.

Scholarships and loans for duly authenticated academic necessities can usually be chiseled from some source even after the budget shows a lean balance, but what every dean needs more than anything else to carry out his merciful obligations is a small reserve fund for which no accounting or explanations have to be made except to his own conscience. He needs it to take care of boys like Dean Briggs' customer with the two left-footed rubbers, like the Hungarian escapee for whom a few meal tickets at the right moment may mean the difference between personal disaster and a bounty of international good will, like Dean Baldwin's Charlie Walters who is in dire want of a friend, counselor, and a ten-dollar loan. It isn't fair to tax the dean personally for all these favors to humanity merely because his position makes him audience to all the hard-luck drama.

Three or four thousand dollars in a "Dean's Purse" can be stretched farther and relieve a greater variety of student anxieties than any scholarship fund of like amount, but deans aren't in a good position to beg for assets accountable only to themselves, and alumni philanthropists

223

seem to overlook this most commendable charity. Stanford is among the few institutions which have such a fund. From it is drawn enough to tide over a promising freshman who returns from Christmas vacation ready to pack up and leave as the result of a sudden crisis in family budgeting. A crack basketball player on the point of dropping from the team because of poor eyesight gets a pair of contact lenses. Twenty dollars goes to a senior who desperately needs a little social relaxation but can't afford a ticket for the senior ball. A check for $150 goes toward repairing a borrowed automobile that has been damaged through no fault of the destitute driver. The fund takes care of unanticipated doctor and dentist bills, minor operations, and pays for several pairs of eyeglasses every year.

The Dean's Purse provides for a kind of alms that cannot come from other, more restricted college funds, and once it is well established, there is no problem of keeping the Purse replenished. Grateful alumni who were once helped through an emergency send back years later twofold or tenfold the cost of a molar extraction, of the fare home, or of a ticket to the senior ball, and friends who hear of the distress miraculously relieved by the timely beneficence of the dean's office are even more generous.

"I wasn't in the right frame of mind to thank you anywhere near properly for pulling out all the stops to lend me the six hundred dollars to fly to England," wrote a British student who had found that the dean's office was the only place he could get immediate financial aid when suddenly summoned home from Stanford. "You didn't bother to trouble me either about how the money was to be repaid. It was due to your prompt kindness that I was able to get here in time to help my mother and to cope generally with the crisis. My father died shortly after I arrived. . . ."

On the other hand, a dejected senior wearing his frayed "scholarship suit" appeared at the dean's office in another college to enter an urgent plea for a five-dollar loan from the "fund." Touched by the suppliant's earnestness, his hungry look, and his hesitancy, the philanthropist reached into his desk drawer for the checkbook. "You're sure five dollars will be enough?" he inquired. The senior assured him that five would take care of the immediate crisis.

As he was about to sign the check, the dean glanced up with the half-embarrassed query: "Bob, what should I note in the records that this is for?"

Without a blink or a blush he answered: "To register my car with the college."

"Car?" exclaimed the dumfounded dean.

"Yes, my new Jaguar."

The fundamental aim of American education is to provide, as nearly as possible, equal opportunities for all classes of students, regardless of economic background. Colleges may not always be able to equalize things with a scholarship, but they can usually help with a job or a loan. Even though it may mean some hard sledding later on, a student shouldn't ignore the dean's suggestion about going into debt, for the statisticians have figured out that the lifetime income of a graduate is $100,000 greater than the expected income of a man without an A.B. In material returns alone it is worth the struggle.

10.

"LOWEST FORM OF ACADEMIC LIFE"

[*The Dean as Scapegoat*]

"TO SERVE EFFICIENTLY," testified Dean Strozier facetiously, "the dean of students should be available, in his office, twenty-four hours a day with no formal appointments, and no backlog of paper work. To serve with safety, he should be disgustingly healthy, imperturbable in time of crisis, benevolent and forgiving when reviled, optimistic and enthusiastic when everything goes wrong. To serve with distinction, he should possess the minor virtues as well: an elephantine memory for names and faces, and the ability to eat and drink anything, anywhere, anytime. . . . Perhaps the highest compliment that can be paid a dean of students at any given time is that he is still a dean of students." [1]

The rate of turnover in contemporary deanships would be alarming to the academic actuary—if there were one. The casualty list is impressive; the mortality table lugubrious. Deans die prematurely. They develop heart disorders, liver trouble, and ulcers. They get trounced in guerrilla warfare with the faculty, come to grief with bumptious members of the board; they are racked, drawn, and quartered by their own presidents, ridden out of town by students. After a year, or two, or three in office they sometimes retreat voluntarily to the department whence they came, sadder and wiser men, or are unvoluntarily booted upstairs to little jobs with big titles. They move from one institution to another in futile search for the ideal student body and the ideal boss. Many a dean who doesn't know how to say "uncle" accepts the lure of a college presidency. Sensing that the hair by which the Damoclean sword hangs is getting too taut, they step aside just before the weapon falls, and enjoy a long, pleasant old age commuting to Madison Avenue or pulling weeds in the garden. As was recounted of one honored knight of the college round table, "He knew that something was wrong, drove his car to the side of the road, turned off the ignition and died." It can all terminate as undramatically as that.

A few deans hold the reins so long they are confused with the institutional founders—possibly because of the layers of awe in which they are encrusted, possibly because they are recognized as a permanent tradition. But there aren't too many of them. Their record for longevity notwithstanding, deaning is a precarious business. Like a football coach who is lauded and lionized until his boys lose their winning streak, the dean may get the preferential treatment for years until something turns sour. Then, overnight, he becomes an illustrious fizzle. Generally coaches and deans have expendability in common.

Every college needs to keep a scapegoat handy, and if the most commonly accepted one can beat his detractor to it, he likes to be the first to pop the old chestnut about the dean's being "the lowest form of academic life," or in self-defense to crack back that the dean is a man who doesn't know enough to be a professor, but knows too much to be a president. He is also familiar with the dubious compliment comparing him to the earthworm that keeps things stirred without being too visible.

"How anyone can envy a dean I would not know," exclaims Dr. Max S. Marshall, professor of microbiology at the University of California Medical Center, who holds the all-time record of serving under twenty-one different deans without becoming one himself. Nevertheless, he realizes that he is among the few in the academic world who doesn't hanker for an appointment to the position. "The gravitational pull is evident," he observes—particularly among "men who want power, have the missionary spirit, love titles, pomp, and ceremony, or dote on committees and organizations. . . . Deans, in short, are amiable fellows with warm handclasps, great understanding and sympathy, and the fishiest eyes in piscatorial records."

Professor Marshall also differentiates between the "firm," strongwilled dean who, for obvious reasons, never lasts long, and the namby-pamby type who adopts the course of expediency and the "idyllic world of unreality," agreeing with all comers. "The dean who does this follows the beam into port, never letting the needle go too far off center. This permits a school to operate, and the dean is never fired because he stays on the shorter end of criticism." [2]

Day in and day out the firm incumbent—the only kind worth his salt—is on a damned-if-you-do and damned-if-you-don't spot, accused of being too soft-hearted by one group and too iron-fisted by another, chided by his superiors for incurring the displeasure of students in cutting short a harmless prank they had planned, and knowing full well that he would have been chided worse if they had been allowed to proceed with their shenanigans; upbraided by the faculty for being too severe with a group of unscrupulous scamps, yet aware that he's getting off lightly considering the censure he would suffer if he hadn't been severe; denounced by undergraduate editors for placing a fraternity on social probation, but unable to explain that if he hadn't taken that action promptly, somebody else would have padlocked the house for keeps.

He is to blame for anything that does go wrong and equally culpable for things that don't go wrong but, by all rules of human conduct, should have. It's the dean's fault when students fail to accept with enthusiasm a new curricular imposition voted by the faculty or a jump in tuition voted by the trustees. For every uprising, every bitter petition, every parental complaint, ultimately he takes the rap.

Then in addition to all this run-of-the-mill reproach—directed for the most part at an "office" rather than an individual—students take singular delight in personal twitting. They may love, honor, and respect their dean, but any such affection doesn't relieve him of having his patience and his sense of humor tried more frequently than would appear necessary. Harvard's beloved Briggs was donning his coat to go out for a late dinner engagement one evening when the doorbell rang. He doffed his coat and welcomed in a group of a dozen expectant underclassmen. No sooner were they settled than the bell rang again and a larger delegation was ushered down the hallway. Shortly every chair in the big house was occupied as more visitors poured in. His embarrassment over the unexpected attention was matched by their apparent anticipation of some extraordinary entertainment—until one of the guests accidentally displayed a copy of the formal printed invitation from "Mr. and Mrs. Briggs" that had been liberally distributed by an anonymous Harvardian.

At Cornell Dean Baldwin listened with interest while a committeeman described a novel contraption invented as the major attraction and moneymaker for the Spring Day Carnival; a target and diving board were being constructed with Rube Goldberg ingenuity on the edge of a capacious water tank so that when a baseball hit the bull's-eye, a wooden arm supporting the board would automatically be released, plunging plank and the man on it into the tank. The student wanted to make sure that there would be no possible objection to the concession, for already a surprising number of marksmen had manifested interest in it.

Dean Baldwin warmly endorsed the contraption and the charitable cause; he predicted that the tank would indeed be a spectacular attraction; complimented the inventor on his skill and the committee on its stratagem in finding a patriot to take the dunkings, and, out of curiosity, inquired who was to play that role.

"Oh, I was just coming to that point," replied the committeeman earnestly. "We already have you advertised for it. We thought you'd be willing to stand on the plank."

In a society that cherishes, cheers, and gives the most nourishment to its yes men, the dean has to be the no man. The answer is *no* to the student who wants to be excused two days before spring vacation to get an early start on a Bermuda tour; it's *no* to parents who think the probation penalty is too severe; *no* to the athletic committee arguing that special scholarship favors should be granted to the football captain. A host is always gathered about his door intent on persuading him to retract the unpalatable *no*. He doesn't like the infernal negative any better than his colleagues, but he has no choice. Just before a holiday recess, when the minds of students are most fertile in contriving artful reasons for special privileges, a dean displayed at his office entrance a poster the size of a theater bill with the single inscription NO. Explanation was unnecessary. His petitioners stared at the sign, grinned, and slunk away.

Yes is a very expensive word for him, for tidings of a single affirmative on an issue of interest to the multitude can spread mysteriously in a forenoon to the uttermost parts of the campus, and pay dividends fiftyfold in similar supplications. One man, for a perfectly logical reason, is granted permission to change the hour of a final examination, and immediately forty others have reasons almost as logical for altering their examination schedules. A needy student is allowed to leave for Christmas holidays four days early to accept a coveted job in his home post office, and impoverished candidates for vacation employment sprout on every side. The authorization of one sophomore salesman to dispense sandwiches in the dormitories is the signal for an army of peddlers to arise, eager to be of service in filling student demands for cigarettes, cokes, magazines, correspondence paper, shaving cream, summer cruises, pinups, ice cream, and haberdashery. *No* is not the soft answer calculated to turn away wrath, but it is the most useful word in the English language for maintaining a semblance of order and organization in the educational establishment. But sometimes the dean wishes that he weren't obliged to hold a monopoly on the word.

While maintaining the negative attitude on the one hand, it is essential that he be instrumental in stirring up a lively college spirit on the other—keep his students cheerful, eager, and shrill in their praise of everything that dear old alma mater does and stands for. He should allow just enough wholesome romping to give the alumni the impression that the place isn't getting dull and going to the dogs, that it is as full of verve and vinegar as it was in their day; and to keep the public entertained, a few antics good for a page-three headline are as important as basketball victories and first-rate commencement oratory.

It is understood that the dean will be the goat in these affairs; he will be lightly ribbed for allowing them to occur, occasionally credited with being a good sport in keeping them confined, roundly condemned if they get out of hand. Someone in the institution has usually gone to the trouble of building up the dean as the man who always takes the side of students, is appreciative and understanding of their ways: he can quickly tell the difference between pranks and perversity. So for events that are clearly nothing more than a vigorous expression of college spirit, the pranksters expect him to look the other way and automatically rush to their defense when the fun degenerates into a tumult.

Amherst was one of the first institutions of higher learning to promote the kind of gang warfare that invariably leaves the dean in a quandary, not knowing whether to ignore or squelch it—interclass or intercollege warfare over some pesky trophy, symbol, or animal more sacred than a Calcutta cow. In 1857 Lieutenant Governor Joel Hayden of Massachusetts presented the college with a curvesome bronze statue of Sabrina in the nude—three hundred pounds of her. For a few seasons she had graced the garden of the Lieutenant Governor's mansion, but it was rumored that the unclothed image of Britain's legendary goddess of the River Severn had proved embarrassing to Mrs. Hayden, and for no good reason other than to placate his wife, the magistrate shipped her to Amherst. It was a mistake from the start. Shocking though she was, Sabrina quickly drew many undergraduate friends. Periodically she acquired lifelike colors representing various races and tribes; more frequently she was provided with attire suitable to the chill Amherst climate. Often she was kidnapped and found tucked between the covers of student cots, or she turned up in unlikely places like the tower of Johnson Chapel, on the roof of the observatory, or at the bottom of the college well.

Finally, in 1884, the President had had enough. He ordered her destroyed. But the solicitous mortuarian in whose care she was placed merely hid the immodest Sabrina in his barn. There she was found three years later by representatives of the class of 1890, who secretly laid plans for returning her to the campus with suitable ceremonies. The operations, however, were thwarted by the class of 1889, who arranged a successful abduction. Then the class of 1891 horned in as she was being conveyed to the college behind a team of horses. Allegedly she spent the following summer at the bottom of the Connecticut River, but by fall the lithesome lady was resuscitated, and thereafter for almost half a century she was at the mercy of rival classes and rival defenders. Conducted from one hiding place to another, she spent a great deal of time in barns, storage bins, bank vaults, and shallow graves. Her travels took her over most of New England and New York. After one conflict she was committed to solitary confinement in a West Virginia coal mine; after another she was incarcerated in the Litchfield, Connecticut, town jail.

The peace-loving class of 1935 at length decided to call a halt to all the nonsense and in 1936 saw her safely soldered to an immovable pedestal in the college museum. For fifteen years she stood there in conspicuous nudity, scarcely paid a sidelong glance. But once more she was liberated, in 1951—severed from her pedestal with the help of an acetylene torch—and for four anxious years she was counted as a casualty, until with country-wide fanfare she was returned for the commencement exercises of 1955. Scarred and bruised in the wrong places after all the abuse, she still appeared to be fit for another century of intergang horseplay. [3]

The feuds over the welfare of Sabrina set a high standard for countless melees that have been the cause of undergraduate bloodshed from coast to coast. Bells and bell clappers, silver trophies, axes, canes, cherished documents, hunks of masonry, fiddles and drums substituted for the

bronze statue, and live mascots ranging from cats to camels and mules to mastiffs were equally popular. At the University of Vermont a half-ton sphere of granite, the "Boulder" which had served for a century and a half as symbol of the institution's durability, disappeared in 1946 from under the noses of masons who were about to cement it into a solid concrete slab. Frantic pleas for its return were answered with unpromising notes of blackmail. From the deep south came a report that the boulder was lodged in a prison rock pile destined to be chipped into bits, unless the University would merge with its rival Norwich; from the midwest that it was about to be run through a stone crusher, but could be retrieved for a price; from upper New York that it was being reshaped to form the cornerstone of a new dormitory; from lower New England that the granite would be pulverized and returned in small envelopes unless the gold and green football jerseys were dyed a suitable shade of crimson. Eventually the plot leaked out that the famed boulder was to be rolled onto the field between halves of the U.V.M.-Middlebury football game. Officials of the rival college visualized the Armageddon that would follow, with bashed heads, broken limbs, and irreparable relations. Negotiators went to work, and instead of being delivered on the football grid, under cover of darkness one night it was rolled onto the neutral territory of the dean's back yard.

A similar bloodletting on the other side of the continent was averted by Dean Byron Atkinson when he learned that his students at UCLA had captured "Tirebiter," the part-Airedale mascot of the University of Southern California; her protectors had hatched a scheme to display the beast from the turret of an armored car between the halves of their annual football classic in the Coliseum, and then release a reasonable facsimile of Tirebiter attached to a helium-filled weather balloon. Just in time Dean Atkinson put his foot down, called off the whole affair, and single-handed prevented a mass transfer of two student bodies to the Los Angeles hospitals.

In the midwest a half-dozen abductors from the University of Kansas almost got away with Kansas State's wildcat: the beast had been successfully shanghaied from its carefully guarded compartment in the Manhattan zoo and was on its way to Lawrence caged on the rear seat of a sedan. But the driver made the mistake of going through a red light, and the car was convoyed to the police station by troopers. Even then they would have gotten away with it, if the kidnappers hadn't possessed such uneasy consciences. Assuming that the police were using the traffic violation only as a ruse for recovering the cat, the moment the driver and his escort entered headquarters, the others raced off with the car and their catch. The nature of the contraband cargo wasn't discovered until an hour later when, thanks to radio, roadblocks, and screaming sirens, another police posse caught up with the escapees. In the small morning hours, an urgent invitation was relayed to the dean of Kansas State to drive some fifty miles to retrieve the snarling animal and prefer charges against the absconders.

The dean at Washington State had a much rougher time recovering the mascot borrowed by University of Idaho students, and the three hijackers, too, went through

237

an even more gruelling experience. "Butch" was a vicious cougar imprisoned behind substantial bars and, for game appearances, was transferred to a traveling cage by a qualified keeper with encouragement from the jet of a hose. But the Idaho rustlers didn't know about the hose. After locating the lair of the cougar, they couldn't persuade the cat to leave her familiar habitat for the inviting chicken-wire crate they had rigged on a pickup truck. So one of the marauders, possessing more courage than wisdom, slipped inside the den. With lashing tail, Butch circled the intruder, screaming defiance and ready to spring, then settled into a corner, glaring fire. It was too late for the student to retreat. Gradually he worked his way behind the animal, with the bold intention of boosting her rump; and, to his surprise, Butch enjoyed the attention, started rubbing against her playmate and acting the part of a purring house cat. Getting scratched behind the ears for the first time in her life was sheer rapture, until puss was suddenly bored by it all, and as a tribute of gratitude, snapped at the hand of the charmer, crunched it to pulp, and obligingly sauntered into the makeshift cage.

For three weeks Washington State's mascot was hospitably cared for in Idaho, but word of her whereabouts filtered back to Pullman, and a contingent of a hundred angry liberators descended upon the Moscow campus, armed with two-foot lengths of metal pipe. The two student bodies lined up for battle, but the clash was averted by the quick thinking of Idaho student leaders. In welcoming addresses, Moscow was declared an open city; the invaders could have complete freedom to prowl and

pry for their lost cat anywhere they wished. The spokes-
men were reasonably sure that the caged cougar—se-
curely hidden in a college barn under a pyramid of
hay bales—would not be discovered. They were right.
The searchers prowled and pried and then returned to
Pullman frustrated and empty-handed.

By that time the personnel administrators of the two
institutions had come to terms, and the dean of Washington State next day backed a paneled truck into the barn,
personally heaved the bales aside, and reclaimed Butch.
He was just clearing the outskirts of the alien campus
when his mission was discovered. A mob descended upon
the truck, wrenching at cab doors, riding the bumpers,
yanking at ignition wires, but the dean kept going, plowed
through the crowd, outdistanced his pursuers, and made
it back to the security of Pullman, where much more interest was shown in the reappearance of Butch than in
the triumph of the dean.

It would be heartwarming, indeed, for a pillar of the
faculty to receive one tenth of the student adulation expended on a campus mutt. Quiet St. Olaf College, for instance, was thrown into a two-day tizzy when an officer
of the law took it upon himself to do away with Ytterboe,
a mongrel mascot that had an insatiable appetite for off-
campus shins. Effigies of the cold-blooded murderer were
burned in the streets; a town-gown riot was soon brewing;
press, radio, and TV joined the fray. Contributions toward a memorial fund for Ytterboe poured in, with
single antes as high as fifty dollars. Before the entire
student body and faculty, assembled on the library lawn,
the dog was appropriately eulogized and the body laid to

239

rest under a splendid blanket of flowers. May 22 was set aside as Ytterboe Day to be observed in perpetuity. In a generous attempt to assuage the grief, rival Carleton College ceremoniously presented the mourners with a fair replica of Ytterboe. No illustrious professor or celebrity in the history of St. Olaf had ever been accorded such honor.

College officials can get very wrought up over these displays of student sentiment, whether the sentiment is seasoned with ferocity or with ordinary facetiousness, for the most light-hearted spree can bubble into a mass orgy. Administratively they are very easily handled: the incident is merely referred to a scapegoat dean with instructions to employ his best judgment. Woe unto him if he misjudges. For his intercessions he is belabored, blacklisted, and blessed, depending on who is affected—but not very often blessed.

As with all off-color college conduct, some Monday-morning philosopher is bound to come up with the suggestion that the fracas could readily have been avoided if the institution only had a law against it: any alert dean should have sense enough to outlaw all mascots, as a crime-prevention measure.

Way back in the recesses of college history, long before presidents had a professional fall guy, experimenting pedagogues evolved a theory that the only sure way to bring student masses under subjection was to have a rule for everything—rules to inspire conformists, rules to terrorize recalcitrants, rules and rewards for exemplary demeanor, rules and penalties for dereliction. Thousands upon thousands of tight-fisted rules littered the pages of college law books, on the order of that ancient regulation at Brown that "No student shall refuse to open his door when he hears the stamp of a foot in the entry." The stamp, decreed the law, was "a token that some officer desires admission, which token every student is forbid to counterfeit or imitate under any pretense whatsoever." [4]

The responding thud of undergraduate feet beating off snow, mud, and insolence echoed in the corridors of Rhode Island halls of learning for generations. Relatively few of the nineteenth-century legal codes survive, but the spirit that made them is uncorrupted. The dean is under attack from the reactionaries for failing to side with them, under a worse barrage from the progressives for not championing their views.

There must be a great many college precepts, but they have never been much more effective in eliminating undergraduate insurgence than was Brown's antistamp act —never much more effective than are civil laws in entirely eliminating city sin and turpitude. Laws don't do the trick, for unfortunately the completely law-abiding citizen is as uncommon on the campus as off. Nevertheless, the lay law-breakers are the first to rally behind the old pedagogues and insist that there are no college problems but couldn't be licked by legislation. As heir to the outworn and outwitted enforcement procedure the dean remains in the middle, trying to fend off the people who are sure that a bad rule is better than no rule. If they had their say, he would still be trudging up and down the corridors stamping a heavy foot outside dormitory doors.

Students can be as baffling to a dean as to anyone else,

241

but the public never has understood them, and the boys, of course, do their level best to make themselves misunderstood. It's part of their game. They prefer to remain aloof and a little superior to the mundane interests of the larger community. Their fashions are foreign, their extracurricular doings are foreign, their acquisitiveness is foreign, their lingo is half unintelligible. A great deal of youthful satisfaction is derived from this befuddlement of their elders, who perennially consider it evidence of a new decadence that college guardians dismiss all too lightly. But there is nothing novel about it. The quaint aloofness of scholars goes back at least to the Middle Ages and was imposed upon the American public as fast as institutions of higher learning were chartered in the colonies.

Undergraduate language alone has been enough to keep outsiders disconcerted. By the time *big shot* as the name for the campus worthy settles into the language, he has become a *wheel* or a *red hot*. A *dig* becomes a *grub*, a *fag*, a *poler*, an *egghead*, and a *dryball;* the *highgo* turns into a *big time*, a *fling*, a *blast*, a *bust*, a *ball*, and an *RF.* The 1920s brought in "Collegiate, Collegiate, Yes, We Are Collegiate," and brought in with it the *wet smacks, sad birds* and *grinds*, and a specialized glossary of terms for *petting, necking,* and *mousing.* But far back in the 1700s and early 1800s the vocabulary was even more colorful, and more varied because of limitations in intercollege communication. A poor response in class was a *stump* at Princeton, a *bull* at Dartmouth, a *barney* at Hamilton and Harvard, a *cork* in the south, a *smash* at Wesleyan;

242

while a dilly of a recitation was a *sail* at Bowdoin, a *shine* or *squirt* at Harvard, a *curl* at the University of Virginia, a *rowl* at Princeton, a *ten-strike* at Hamilton, and a *blood* in colleges to the west. To cheat or plagiarize was known as *skinning*, and the nice word for dishonest interlining of translation in the Greek or Latin text was *illuminating*. Pleasantries for outhouses ran from *temples* at Bowdoin to *johns* at Union, *Cousins* or *Cuz-johns* at Harvard, *joes* at Yale and Hamilton, *No. 10s* or *No. 1001s* at Wesleyan and the University of Vermont.

By 1851 the collegians had introduced so much alien terminology into the English language that John Bartlett felt called upon to publish a special lexicon of undergraduate speech. The discordant lingo, of course, is only symbolic of the greater differences between town and gown. Add to this the collision in points of view, the rebel spirit, the wearing jocularity, the affected preoccupation with sophistry, and the two societies have little in common. None of the dean's predecessors was ever very successful in breaking down the barriers, and the contemporary arbiter cannot claim much progress either. Presumably one of his present responsibilities is to act as interpreter and peacemaker for these foreign communities. He dutifully attends Rotary Club meetings every Thursday, accepts membership on Chamber of Commerce committees, addresses the DAR chapter, and the Parent-Teacher Association, but while he is translating one psychological quirk of his students, they are off on another tangent. He is stuck with a Sisyphean task, the townsfolk assailing him for allowing the boys to be so devious, the boys chuckling at his naïve attempts to keep pace. It is unlikely that the twain shall ever meet through any of his efforts at mediation.

Colleges seem to have taken on more responsibility than they are able to carry, observe the townsmen. Ostensibly the institutions of learning have been set up as factories scheduled to produce the leaders of tomorrow; their catalogues brag of efficient production lines, their alumni magazines toast the brilliant successes of graduates, the literature for million-dollar fund drives promises to supply more like them if subscribers will give generously toward bigger laboratories, libraries, and basketball floors. Yet somehow in the process of all this production, complain critical laymen, the prospective leaders of tomorrow are not setting a very good example for younger juveniles of today; the absorption in unacademic frills, in speed and sports, in parties and protests, in beer and barbarisms, is being handed on to the secondary schools while the college pace-setters are taking to more exotic forms of amusement. The dean can't be held blameless.

Certainly the townsfolk have ample circumstantial evidence to back their slurs. Perhaps the colleges aren't doing so well; perhaps the publicists have overexaggerated the accomplishment, and the idealists have cut out too large an order for higher education. Dean Gauss was one of those who thought so twenty years ago. "At a critical period in the history of higher education in America," he remarked, "when we were not quite certain what the aim of a college should be, we invented the labor-saving but mischievous phrase 'education for leadership.' It is, of course, of the highest importance that in a democracy there should be men of sterling character to whom their fellows will look for guidance, but such character and such leadership are and always must be by-products of useful and devoted lives. . . . We have put the cart before the horse and must unhitch and start over again. We must begin the necessary process of deflating higher education. One of our first steps . . . will be to get rid of this unfortunate and often pernicious nonsense about leadership." [5]

Undoubtedly purveyors of education from the junior college through graduate school have allowed students to construct false values for assessing qualities of leadership. Personality, agreeableness, conformity, and social finesse have been elevated above creativity and scholarly achievement. The tendency has been to measure leadership more in terms of the extracurriculum than of the classroom. And deans, who are in a position to help set the tone of the institution, have been as guilty as any of their colleagues in cultivating the false values. Since a satisfied, compliant student body is easier to manage than an animated one, they have been more concerned with social contentment than intellectual stimulation. They have neglected educational priorities, deemphasized the superior standard of scholarship in their enthusiasm for development of the "whole man," and overlooked Jacques Barzun's precept that "the only thing worth teaching anybody is a principle."

The extracurriculum would chuck into place naturally enough if the curriculum were first set solidly where it ought to be, and if there were a little less protective solicitude for the social adjustments. Benefits to be derived

245

from instruction in the department of hard knocks have been all but disregarded. Forgetting that a man has sooner or later to gain moral strength from the disappointment and pain of not being among those chosen, deans are inclined, for instance, to condemn a fraternity rushing system which provides that experience. Too much effort is expended on making things run too smoothly.

A student who arrives ready and willing to be plunged immediately into the rigors of a tough class schedule is let down by the discovery that his mentors consider him incapable of facing it until he has been properly conditioned. Mass "orientation" programs are planned to help freshmen settle comfortably and congenially into their new environment, yet the impression inadvertently left by the agenda is that the college is more concerned with introducing its recreational facilities than its cultural opportunities.

The anti-intellectual atmosphere of residence halls and fraternity houses is deplored, but tolerated. Deans have observed that the student who has a consuming interest in a subject isn't bothered about how difficult it is, stays out of trouble, and doesn't have much use for either the counseling bureau or the psychiatrist, but they have not too frequently applied the principles gathered from that observation in recommending therapeutic treatment for the troublemakers, the malcontents, and the playboys. Searching for novel or clinical means of bringing out qualities of leadership, they have overlooked Dean Gauss' very simple truth that genuine leadership is "a by-product of useful and devoted lives."

In the college family of administrators the dean is often

the uncongenial member in accepting the course of expediency for undergraduates, but by weight of votes he is forced to go along. He cannot afford always to be the rebel. "Perhaps we have emphasized getting along harmoniously with other people too much," challenges one self-critical dean. "That over-emphasis frequently acts as an excuse for the lack of courage to face real issues and to take stands which, though supported by sound educational principles, may result in unpleasant situations. . . . Neither facts nor consequences of ideas are always pleasant, but those who work in the academic community owe their first obligation to facts and ideas." [6]

According to the surveys of educational apologists, students have been getting progressively more civilized and more addicted to culture for centuries, their conduct is steadily improving, their seriousness of purpose growing more serious. To prove it the probers have only to cite statistics or produce unflattering illustrations from some previous generation. Deans are in the ranks of these optimists, loyally defending the aspirations of their clientele, but they are scared about a future when there will be an additional three million to look after.

"There is real danger," warns President Spathelf, "that we shall succumb to the demands and evils of mass production in higher education. The inevitable danger in the handling of large numbers of people is that we lose sight of the individual and his needs. Large classes, doubled-up lecture sections, extended instructional days and class schedules, improvisation of space, expansion of facilities, mass testing and counseling devices, fewer intimate student contacts are all going to legislate against the in-

247

dividual. These are not fancied possibilities, they have been past realities. They are future threats. The student who distinguishes himself in attainment will still be noticed, as probably will the student who fails, but the size of the 'lost battalion'—that great number of students who fall in neither extreme and who are apt to go unnoticed, will surely increase."

There will indeed be a new order for the student of the next decade, and it is quite possible that he will have a different kind of dean to deal with. In one of those typically American shifts in temperament, people who had never before shown much interest in education were demanding that the martinet move back into the administrator's chair, that he shake off some of the smooth educational jargon, the soft chastisement, the complacency, and the "pedaguese." Anyone who had ever crossed a campus discovered that he knew what was wrong with education, and was ready to sound off. The most familiar theme was a gospel of coercion: it was high time that students got down to business and were made to study what was good for them; at least get the dullards out of the way and give the bright boys a chance to expand.

The emphasis on coercion, however, didn't originate with the schoolmen. It came from the parents of students, their uncles, aunts, and literate cousins. Increasingly they had been made aware of the "crisis in education" growing out of overpopulated classrooms, the threat of far worse crowding, and the dearth of instructors. But the hysteria of interest came in the wake of a man-made satellite launched from Russian soil. The gospel of coercion was branded on the public conscience on the night the world was abruptly thrust into the age of space.

"Scientific Triumph of Russia Shows a Paradox in Education!"—"Has Sputnik Taught Us a Lesson?"—"Our Educational Complacency Has Been Shattered: Where Do We Go From Here?" echoed the press from coast to coast as the stunning truth of our curricular shortcomings, compared to Soviet educational successes, was brought to light. Newspapers and news magazines, literary journals, religious, scientific, and business monthlies, periodicals varying in type from the *Wall Street Journal* to *Nature Magazine* jumped on the bandwagon to lambaste an educational system editors had been lauding only a few days before.

In consternation the titles of the treatises often overshadowed the text. Week by week they built up a caustic crescendo: "Russia Rings the School Bell"—"Cold War Comes to the Classroom"—"Challenge Is Ours"—"Rough Road to Outer Space"—"Education for the Defense of America"—"Education for the Long Run"—"Money is Not Enough"—"Education Needs More than Cash and Crash"—"Change the Thinking"—"Spirit Is Lacking"— "We Are Less Educated Than Fifty Years Ago"—"A Nation of Advanced Plumbers"—"Wake Up the Educators" —"We Cannot Sleep"—"Do American Educators Know What They Are Up To?"—"Panic Among the Educators!"

To the public the incredible revelation that Soviet laboratories could turn out scientific miracles that competed with American ingenuity represented a catastrophe worse than Pearl Harbor, and the realization that a foreign system of education produced results we couldn't match was a scandalous national humiliation. Convinced that a cold war of scholarship could go on for a generation or two, alarmists concluded that the only route to survival was the route of classroom compulsion.

The pressure was on. Deans were as much to blame for letting the Russians get the jump on us as any of the other educational bigwigs. "Administrators must learn to appreciate scholarship by working at it," cried the critics, tired of reading about tolerance toward slow starters and cougar-tamers; the educational system needed to be tightened up, and the best man to do the tightening was the scientist or the humanist who could exemplify the rugged, demanding discipline he expected in his students; the paragon in the dean's office would set a better example if he were a scholar and a man of ideas trained in science, letters, and philosophy, rather than in dormitory management, social planning, and psychological guidance. The citadels of pedagogy obviously were not producing the right kind of leadership.

Sparks that Sputnik dropped on every campus in the country were hard to stamp out. They flared up in alumni circles, in faculty and committee meetings, in the corridors of the administration building, in the dean's office. Things would never be the same again. But any demand for a bruising shakeup in personnel administration isn't quite realistic. The disciplinary dean and the counseling dean will patch up their differences, and both will be obliged to reshape their ideas to incorporate the philosophy of coercion—with less emphasis on academic ease and cultural complacency. In the college that manages to remain small and independent there will be room for the deanly scholar, but the booming university will have to reserve the big chair for the organization man, the impersonal personnel specialist whose first responsibility is managing the masses instead of the individual. The very nature of a cumbersome student body and the unwieldy university colossus makes his professional services essential.

The undergraduate of the next decade undoubtedly faces a harder grind, tougher competition, severer stricture, and as the avalanche of collegians such as has never been known in any country in any age descends upon the campus, most of the flummery about the permissive attitude and the progressive approach will be lost in the shuffle. Readjustment will take a long time, but it is clear that a new era of rigor and regulation is coming in, and the dean will be called on once again to swing the strap.

Bend over, son.

QUOTATION SOURCES

Chapter 1.—1. Berkeley (Calif.) *Daily Gazette,* Nov. 15, 1957, p. 1—2. *Nation,* Nov. 13, 1913, p. 457—3. Secretarial Notes, Nineteenth Annual Conference, National Association of Deans and Advisers of Men (NADAM), 1937, p. 118.

Chapter 2.—1. B. A. Hall, *A Collection of College Words and Customs,* p. 92—2. *Ibid.,* pp. 81-82—3. *Ibid.,* p. 5—4. *Ibid.,* p. 76—5. *Ibid.,* pp. 27, 61-63—6. NADAM (1937), p. 111—7. W. S. Tyler, *Higher Education of Women* (Educational Discourses)—8. NADAM (1937), p. 116—9. Rollo Walter Brown, *Dean Briggs* (New York: Harper & Bros., 1926), p. 100.

Chapter 3.—1. N. M. Clark, "Thousands of Young Men Tell 'Tommy Arkle' Their Troubles," *American Magazine* (January 1925), pp. 19 ff. —2. Christian Gauss, *Life in College* (New York: Charles Scribner's Sons, 1930)—3. Thomas A. Clark, *Discipline and the Derelict* (New York: The Macmillan Company, 1922), p. 77.

Chapter 4.—1. Proceedings, Thirty-ninth Anniversary Conference, National Association of Student Personnel Administrators (NASPA), 1957, p. 184—2. *Ibid.,* 1954, p. v.—3. NADAM (1933), pp. 73-82—4. Fred H. Turner, "Students of the Depression," *Saturday Evening Post* (February 2, 1935), pp. 12-13—5. NADAM (1944), pp. 26-30—6. NADAM (1946), pp. 24-26.

Chapter 5.—1. NADAM (1933), pp. 118-20—2. Brown, *op. cit.,* p. 101 —3. NADAM (1951), p. 29—4. Gauss, *op. cit.,* p. 148—5. NADAM (1933), p. 44—6. NASPA (1953), p. 9—7. H. E. Hawkes and A. L. R. Hawkes, *Through a Dean's Open Door* (New York: McGraw-Hill Book Co., Inc., 1945), p. 17—8. N. M. Clark, *op. cit.,* p. 76—9. E. C. Wil-

252

liamson (ed.), *Trends in Student Personnel Work* (Minneapolis: University of Minnesota Press, 1949), p. 22—10. Hawkes and Hawkes, *op. cit.*, p. 37.

Chapter 6.—1. "What Makes a Committee Tick," *Business Week* (March 20, 1954), pp. 42-48—2. NASPA (1957), p. 219—3. M. S. Marshall, "How to Be a Dean," *AAUP Bulletin* (Winter 1956), p. 640—4. *Christian Century* (November 5, 1952), p. 1280—5. R. M. Strozier, "Oldest Living Dean," *University of Chicago Magazine* (April 1956), pp. 8-10 —6. NASPA (1956), pp. 78-80—7. *Ibid.*, pp. 158-59—8. C. Gilbert Wrenn, *Student Personnel Work in College* (New York: The Ronald Press Co., 1951), p. 269—9. NASPA (1955), pp. 37-38—10. NASPA (1956), pp. 38-41—11. NASPA (1955), pp. 31-33—12. Strozier, *op. cit.*, p. 10—13. NASPA (1956), p. 91.

Chapter 7.—1. "Confessions of a College Dean," *New Republic* (June 22, 1927), pp. 117-19—2. E. J. Durnall, *Personnel and Guidance Journal* (February 1956), pp. 376-77.—3. E. G. Williamson, *ibid.* (October 1955), p. 74—4. T. H. Shrewsbury, "What's Your Verdict?" *ibid.* (March 1956), p. 448—5. Gauss, *op. cit.*, p. 219—6. *Daily Californian*, May 17, 1956; June 5, 1956. Berkeley City Police Department, *University of California Student Disturbances, May 1956, Report and Recommendations*—7. NASPA (1956), pp. 231-32—8. NASPA (1957), p. 124—9. NASPA (1957), pp. 49-50.

Chapter 8.—1. Case histories from Institute for College and University Administrators, Harvard Business School—2. NASPA (1957), pp. 109-10—3. H. J. L. Stark in NADAM (1937), p. 7—4. R. M. Strozier in NASPA (1954), p. 28.

Chapter 9.—1. "Study Now, Pay Later," *Fortune* (May 1956), p. 96—2. *College Admissions 4*, "The Student from School to College," (New York: C. E. E. B. 1957), pp. 85-86—3. D. J. Malcolm, "Working His Way Through College," *Harvard Alumni Bulletin* (June 11, 1925).

Chapter 10.—1. Strozier, "Oldest Living Dean," *op. cit.*, p. 8—2. Marshall, *op. cit.*, pp. 636-37—3. *The New York Times* (June 12, 1955), p. 112—4. *Literary Digest* (May 26, 1934), p. 34—5. Gauss, *op. cit.*, pp. 136-37—6. Strozier in NASPA (1954), p. 25—7. Spathelf in NASPA (1953), p. 38—8. "Graduate Degrees in Education," *School and Society* (January 18, 1958), p. 43.

Quotations not cited above are from interviews or personal correspondence with deans.

INDEX

Index